Business Guides on the Go

"Business Guides on the Go" presents cutting-edge insights from practice on particular topics within the fields of business, management, and finance. Written by practitioners and experts in a concise and accessible form the series provides professionals with a general understanding and a first practical approach to latest developments in business strategy, leadership, operations, HR management, innovation and technology management, marketing or digitalization. Students of business administration or management will also benefit from these practical guides for their future occupation/careers.

These Guides suit the needs of today's fast reader.

Mihail Busu

Essentials of Investment and Risk Analysis

Theory and Applications

Mihail Busu
Bucharest University of Economic Studies
București, Romania

ISSN 2731-4758   ISSN 2731-4766 (electronic)
Business Guides on the Go
ISBN 978-3-031-15055-5   ISBN 978-3-031-15056-2 (eBook)
https://doi.org/10.1007/978-3-031-15056-2

© The Editor(s) (if applicable) and The Author(s), under exclusive licence to Springer Nature Switzerland AG 2022

This work is subject to copyright. All rights are solely and exclusively licensed by the Publisher, whether the whole or part of the material is concerned, specifically the rights of translation, reprinting, reuse of illustrations, recitation, broadcasting, reproduction on microfilms or in any other physical way, and transmission or information storage and retrieval, electronic adaptation, computer software, or by similar or dissimilar methodology now known or hereafter developed.

The use of general descriptive names, registered names, trademarks, service marks, etc. in this publication does not imply, even in the absence of a specific statement, that such names are exempt from the relevant protective laws and regulations and therefore free for general use.

The publisher, the authors, and the editors are safe to assume that the advice and information in this book are believed to be true and accurate at the date of publication. Neither the publisher nor the authors or the editors give a warranty, expressed or implied, with respect to the material contained herein or for any errors or omissions that may have been made. The publisher remains neutral with regard to jurisdictional claims in published maps and institutional affiliations.

This Springer imprint is published by the registered company Springer Nature Switzerland AG.
The registered company address is: Gewerbestrasse 11, 6330 Cham, Switzerland

Contents

1 **Introduction**   1
   References   5

2 **Time Value of Money**   11
   2.1   Simple Interest   14
        2.1.1   Solved Problems   15
        2.1.2   Applications   18
   2.2   Compound Interest   19
        2.2.1   Solved Problems   21
        2.2.2   Applications   27

3 **Financial Markets**   29
   3.1   Monetary Market   30
   3.2   Capital Market   36
        3.2.1   Instruments Presented on the Capital Market   41
        3.2.2   Solved Problems   44
        3.2.3   Applications   45

4 Stock Market — 51
- 4.1 Value and Price of the Stocks — 54
- 4.2 Stock Valuation — 59
  - 4.2.1 Solved Problems — 63
  - 4.2.2 Applications — 65
- 4.3 Dividend Valuation Models — 67
  - 4.3.1 Zero Growth Model — 69
  - 4.3.2 Constant Growth Model — 70
  - 4.3.3 Multiple Growth Model — 71
- 4.4 Valuation Based on a Finite Holding Period — 73
  - 4.4.1 Solved Problems — 77
  - 4.4.2 Applications — 79

5 Bond Market — 83
- 5.1 Bond Structure — 85
- 5.2 Types of Bonds — 87
  - 5.2.1 International Bonds — 90
- 5.3 Clauses Associated with the Bonds — 92
- 5.4 Additional Rights — 94
- 5.5 Factors that Influence and Determine the Value of Bonds — 95
- 5.6 Financial Evaluation of the Bonds — 97
  - 5.6.1 Solved Problems — 99
  - 5.6.2 Applications — 102

6 Portfolio Theory — 105
- 6.1 One and Two-Stock Portfolios — 105
  - 6.1.1 Risk and Return of a Portfolio — 107
  - 6.1.2 Solved Problems — 108
  - 6.1.3 Applications — 111
- 6.2 Three-Stock Portfolios — 113
  - 6.2.1 Solved Problems — 114
  - 6.2.2 Applications — 117
- 6.3 Efficient Portfolios Consisting of Two Risky Assets — 118
  - 6.3.1 Minimum Risk for a Fixed Return — 118
  - 6.3.2 Solved Problems — 120

	6.3.3	Maximum Return	123
	6.3.4	Solved Problems	124
	6.3.5	Applications	125

7 Derivatives 127
7.1 Options 133
7.2 Standardized Options 134
7.2.1 Interest Rate Contracts 135
7.3 CALL Option 140
7.4 PUT Option 142
7.5 Option Strategies 144
7.5.1 Strategies for Hedge 144
7.5.2 Options Trading Strategies on Spread 145
7.5.3 Strategies Using Combinations of Call and Options Put 149

8 Summary Problems 151

1

Introduction

The importance of the topic lies in the fact that it approaches the capital market segment, which has evolutionary theoretical meanings and major practical implications, deriving from the complex relationships between the allocation of available resources and the efficient and optimal use of capital demand in an economy (Kumar, 1996; Ghosh et al., 2007; Abramov et al., 2015). The existence and the degree of development of the capital market has also become for our national economy a criterion and a condition, a standard of the degree of evolution and development of the functional market economy (Paulsen, 1998; Benjamin et al., 2001; Kim et al., 2017).

Placing ourselves in the realm of theoretical approaches, any new research in the field of financial theory is important, starting from the modern investments and risk theory of portfolio theory (Gordon-Shapiro, Markowitz, and Sharpe theories) (Richardson & Mapp, 1976; Roger, 2004; Sandsmark & Vennemo, 2007), but also in terms of its recent evolutions (linear and nonlinear models) (Rosenzweig & Binswanger, 1992; Weitzman, 2012; Talarico & Reniers, 2016).

The book is structured into six chapters: "Time value of money," "Financial Markets," "The Capital Market," "Stock Market," "Bonds Market," and "Portfolio Theory."

The time value of money is a basic financial concept that holds that money in the present is worth more than the same sum of money to be received in the future (Graeme & James, 1996; Mason & Harrison, 2004). This is true because money that you have right now can be invested and earn a return, thus creating a larger amount of money in the future.

The financial market consists of three major sectors, three distinct markets: the banking market, the money market and the capital market. The concept, the main features, functions as well as the structure of the capital market were further captured. The capital market represents the set of relations and mechanisms through which the available and dispersed capitals of the economy are directed to the enterprises or to any public and private entities that request funds (Lintner, 1969; Cohen et al., 2013; Pedersen et al., 2014).

The capital market deals with transactions with medium and long-term financial assets, through them ensuring the transfers of available capital to users whose needs exceed the domestic coverage possibilities. The main motivation of a capital market lies in the economy and the placement of securities of the companies seeking capital potential investors, holders of capital surpluses (Wang & Wu, 2001; Ho & Ho, 2006; Munoz et al., 2009).

The stock market broadly refers to the collection of exchanges and other venues where the buying, selling, and issuance of shares of publicly held companies take place. Such financial activities are conducted through institutionalized formal exchanges (whether physical or electronic) or via over-the-counter (OTC) marketplaces that operate under a defined set of regulations (Demmel & Askin, 1996; Brunette & Couture, 2008; Angelopoulos et al., 2017).

The bond market (also debt market or credit market) is a financial market where participants can issue new debt, known as the primary market, or buy and sell debt securities, known as the secondary market (Højgaard & Taksar, 2001; Leippold et al., 2007).

The concept of portfolio theory was further approached, viewed through the prism of the theoretical approach of the complex universe of theories in this field.

The investment process has many faces: it can involve investing money in bonds, common stock, property, or any other asset; it may involve speculative stocks in a rising market or short sales in a falling market; it may involve the choice of "growth" or "value" shares, the choice of bonds, options, and other financial securities; it can lead to the accumulation of funds or the dissipation of resources. Diversity and competition are the main attributes of this effervescent domain (Klausner, 1969; Kumar, 1996; Schied, 2007).

In all this labyrinth, an important place is occupied by the portfolio management, both from a theoretical point of view and from a practical point of view. Individual investors, fund managers, and institutional investors must decide on the objectives to be pursued and, depending on them, select from the possible investment alternatives (Shevchenko et al., 2008; Cejnek & Randl, 2016; Tryhuba et al., 2021).

The desideratum of the investment act assumes certain fundamental options. As part of the risk control mechanism, the decision must be made based on the selection of multiple assets in order to build a portfolio that balances the two fundamental elements, risk and return (Amit et al., 1990; Patel & Chrisman, 2014).

Another element that will determine the success of the investment is the time horizon; choosing a short-, medium-, or long-term investment can lead to an advantageous gain or, if the choice is not based on portfolio management theories and techniques, to a loss situation (Baietti & Raymond, 2005; Bucciol et al., 2019).

Therefore, the theory and practice of portfolio management is a recognition of the personal needs and lifestyle of the individual investor and a recognition of the institutional imperatives of professional investors (pension funds, investment banks, investment funds, etc.). Both categories of investors need to know that this complex market requires knowledge of risk control techniques and real capital assessment (Dos Santos, 2003; Gómez-Fuster & Jiménez, 2020).

If people are risk averse, they will make the decision to buy an asset based on both the expected future income and the analysis of the risk associated with that gain. Under the influence of risk aversion, for example, investors will want to hold bonds valued in different currencies if the resulting financial asset portfolio provides the desired combination of risk and gain, even if the interest rates offered by those bonds are eroded by currency parities. In general, a portfolio whose earnings fluctuate sharply year after year is less desirable than a portfolio that offers the same earnings year after year, with minor fluctuations (Cubbage et al., 2010; Filippova et al., 2014).

The conclusion is that risk is seen as a phenomenon that comes from circumstances for which the decision maker can identify possible developments and even the probability of their materialization, without being able to specify exactly which of these events will actually occur. It can be stated that the risk comes from the impossibility to assess with a certain accuracy which is the possible event, identified as such by the decision maker and which will materialize and will determine a certain level of risk. Even if the estimated probability for the effective materialization of a certain risk-generating factor is high, the decision maker cannot be sure if that event is the one that will occur with certainty and not another; it is even possible to produce a phenomenon whose probability was estimated at a low level or even an unforeseen event (Lintner, 1975; Elmiger & Kim, 2003; Ambrus et al., 2014).

There is a wide variety of investment risks; each of them being determined by certain risk-generating factors, has certain components and forms of materialization that produce the most varied effects. It is important for investors to identify as many of these aspects as possible for a more correct substantiation of the investment decision (Panicker et al., 2019).

From the investor's point of view, the main attraction of the two strategies is the same: reducing risk through diversification. By holding many shares, representing several industries and market sectors, investors hope to create a protective blanket against major losses that could occur if they had all the money invested in a certain area that would have suffered a disaster (Paulsen & Gjessing, 1997). Under normal circumstances (according to the theory), some stocks in a diversified fund will decrease, while others will increase and hopefully the latter will offset losses. Active managers believe that the chances increase as the number of shares in the portfolio increases (Redmond & Cubbage, 1988; Burja & Burja, 2009; Sagi, 2021).

Market synchronization has long been one of the biggest problems for investors. Acquisition of financial securities at excessively high prices limits the gains that can be obtained; also, selling financial securities in the portfolio at a low price can lead to losses. However, the prices of financial securities fluctuate and the behavior of investors sometimes causes their reactions to be in total opposition to the activities they should engage in to benefit from these fluctuations (Godfrey & Espinosa, 1996). Ideally, investors should buy when prices are low and sell when prices of financial securities rise (Chung, 1991). But investors are usually reluctant to buy when prices fall, fearing that prices will fall further or fearing that prices will not rise in the future (Morse, 1998; Li et al., 2013). When the prices of financial securities are very high, investors are reluctant to sell, because they wish to maximize their profits and feel that prices will rise even more in the future (Sharp, 1991; Thompson, 1997). Special discipline is needed to be able to buy when the prices of financial securities are low and pessimism is present on the market and to be able to sell when the prices of financial securities are high and an exaggerated optimism is felt in the market (de Beus et al., 2003; Jegadeesh et al., 2009; Bitsch et al., 2010).

The book is addressed primarily to students of universities with Economics education profile, which targets the essential aspects related to the investments, risk and portfolio theory and the issue of financial investments to be studied in the first cycle of education, respectively Bachelor.

The book can be also studied by other specialists interested in the field of investment and risk theory or by future master students, respectively doctoral students, who have graduated other faculties than Economics.

References

Abramov, A., Radygin, A., & Chernova, M. (2015). Long-term portfolio investments: New insight into return and risk. *Russian Journal of Economics, 1*(3), 273–293.

Ambrus, A., Chandrasekhar, A. G., & Elliott, M. (2014). *Social investments, informal risk sharing, and inequality* (No. w20669). National Bureau of Economic Research.

Amit, R., Glosten, L., & Muller, E. (1990). Entrepreneurial ability, venture investments, and risk sharing. *Management Science, 36*(10), 1233–1246.

Angelopoulos, D., Doukas, H., Psarras, J., & Stamtsis, G. (2017). Risk-based analysis and policy implications for renewable energy investments in Greece. *Energy Policy, 105*, 512–523.

Baietti, A., & Raymond, P. (2005). *Financing water supply and sanitation investments: Utilizing risk mitigation instruments to bridge the financing gap.*

Benjamin, J., Sirmans, S., & Zietz, E. (2001). Returns and risk on real estate and other investments: More evidence. *Journal of Real Estate Portfolio Management, 7*(3), 183–214.

Bitsch, F., Buchner, A., & Kaserer, C. (2010). Risk, return and cash flow characteristics of infrastructure fund investments. *EIB Papers, 15*(1), 106–136.

Brunette, M., & Couture, S. (2008). Public compensation for windstorm damage reduces incentives for risk management investments. *Forest Policy and Economics, 10*(7–8), 491–499.

Bucciol, A., Cavasso, B., & Zarri, L. (2019). Can risk averse households make risky investments? The role of trust in others. *The Scandinavian Journal of Economics, 121*(1), 326–352.

Burja, C., & Burja, V. (2009). The risk analysis for investments projects decision. *Annales Universitatis Apulensis: Series Oeconomica, 11*(1), 98.

Cejnek, G., & Randl, O. (2016). Risk and return of short-duration equity investments. *Journal of Empirical Finance, 36*, 181–198.

Chung, T. Y. (1991). Incomplete contracts, specific investments, and risk sharing. *The Review of Economic Studies, 58*(5), 1031–1042.

Cohen, D. A., Dey, A., & Lys, T. Z. (2013). Corporate governance reform and executive incentives: Implications for investments and risk taking. *Contemporary Accounting Research, 30*(4), 1296–1332.

Cubbage, F., Koesbandana, S., Mac Donagh, P., Rubilar, R., Balmelli, G., Olmos, V. M., et al. (2010). Global timber investments, wood costs, regulation, and risk. *Biomass and Bioenergy, 34*(12), 1667–1678.

de Beus, P., Bressers, M., & de Graaf, T. (2003). Alternative investments and risk measurement. In *Proceedings 13th AFIR International Colloquium Maastricht/Niederlande* (Vol. 1, pp. 293–307).

Demmel, J. G., & Askin, R. G. (1996). Multiobjective evaluation of advanced manufacturing system technology investments with risk. *IIE Transactions, 28*(3), 249–259.

Dos Santos, B. L. (2003). Information technology investments: Characteristics, choices, market risk and value. *Information Systems Frontiers, 5*(3), 289–301.

Elmiger, G., & Kim, S. S. (2003). *Riskgrade your investments: Measure your risk and create wealth*. Wiley.

Filippova, I. A., Khairullin, I. G., & Usanova, D. S. (2014). Risk-oriented technique of real investments management: Concepts. *Mediterranean Journal of Social Sciences, 5*(24), 11–11.

Ghosh, A., Moon, D., & Tandon, K. (2007). CEO ownership and discretionary investments. *Journal of Business Finance & Accounting, 34*(5–6), 819–839.

Godfrey, S., & Espinosa, R. (1996). A practical approach to calculating costs of equity for investments in emerging markets. *Journal of Applied Corporate Finance, 9*(3), 80–90.

Gómez-Fuster, J. M., & Jiménez, P. (2020). Probabilistic risk modelling for port investments: A practical approach. *Case Studies on Transport Policy, 8*(3), 822–831.

Graeme, N., & James, W. (1996). Assessing risk for international real estate investments. *Journal of Real Estate Research, 11*(2), 103–115.

Ho, M. W., & Ho, K. H. D. (2006). Risk management in large physical infrastructure investments: The context of seaport infrastructure development and investment. *Maritime Economics & Logistics, 8*(2), 140–168.

Højgaard, B., & Taksar, M. (2001). Optimal risk control for a large corporation in the presence of returns on investments. *Finance and Stochastics, 5*(4), 527–547.

Jegadeesh, N., Kräussl, R., & Pollet, J. (2009). *Risk and expected returns of private equity investments: Evidence based on market prices* (No. w15335). National Bureau of Economic Research.

Kim, K., Mithas, S., & Kimbrough, M. (2017). Information technology investments and firm risk across industries: Evidence from the bond market. *MIS Quarterly, 41*(4), 1347–1367.

Klausner, R. F. (1969). The evaluation of risk in marine capital investments. *The Engineering Economist, 14*(4), 183–214.

Kumar, R. L. (1996). A note on project risk and option values of investments in information technologies. *Journal of Management Information Systems, 13*(1), 187–193.

Leippold, M., Wu, L., & Egloff, D. (2007). Variance risk dynamics, variance risk premia, and optimal variance swap investments. In *EFA 2006 Zurich meetings paper*.

Li, Z., Roshandeh, A. M., Zhou, B., & Lee, S. H. (2013). Optimal decision making of interdependent tollway capital investments incorporating risk and uncertainty. *Journal of Transportation Engineering, 139*(7), 686–696.

Lintner, J. (1969). The valuation of risk assets and the selection of risky investments in stock portfolios and capital budgets: A reply. *The Review of Economics and Statistics*, 222–224.

Lintner, J. (1975). The valuation of risk assets and the selection of risky investments in stock portfolios and capital budgets. In *Stochastic optimization models in finance* (pp. 131–155). Academic Press.

Mason, C., & Harrison, R. (2004). Does investing in technology-based firms involve higher risk? An exploratory study of the performance of technology and non-technology investments by business angels. *Venture Capital: An International Journal of Entrepreneurial Finance, 6*(4), 313–332.

Morse, W. C. (1998). Risk taking in personal investments. *Journal of Business and Psychology, 13*(2), 281–288.

Munoz, J. I., Contreras, J., Caamano, J., & Correia, P. F. (2009, June). Risk assessment of wind power generation project investments based on real options. In *2009 IEEE Bucharest PowerTech* (pp. 1–8). IEEE.

Panicker, V. S., Mitra, S., & Upadhyayula, R. S. (2019). Institutional investors and international investments in emerging economy firms: A behavioral risk perspective. *Journal of World Business, 54*(4), 322–334.

Patel, P. C., & Chrisman, J. J. (2014). Risk abatement as a strategy for R&D investments in family firms. *Strategic Management Journal, 35*(4), 617–627.

Paulsen, J. (1998). Sharp conditions for certain ruin in a risk process with stochastic return on investments. *Stochastic Processes and their Applications, 75*(1), 135–148.

Paulsen, J., & Gjessing, H. K. (1997). Optimal choice of dividend barriers for a risk process with stochastic return on investments. *Insurance: Mathematics and Economics, 20*(3), 215–223.

Pedersen, N., Page, S., & He, F. (2014). Asset allocation: Risk models for alternative investments. *Financial Analysts Journal, 70*(3), 34–45.

Redmond, C. H., & Cubbage, F. W. (1988). Portfolio risk and returns from timber asset investments. *Land Economics, 64*(4), 325–337.

Richardson, J. W., & Mapp, H. P. (1976). Use of probabilistic cash flows in analyzing investments under conditions of risk and uncertainty. *Journal of Agricultural and Applied Economics, 8*(2), 19–24.

Roger, B. (2004). Risk and private real estate investments. *Journal of Real Estate Portfolio Management, 10*(2), 113–127.

Rosenzweig, M. R., & Binswanger, H. P. (1992). *Wealth, weather risk, and the composition and profitability of agricultural investments* (Vol. 1055). World Bank Publications.

Sagi, J. S. (2021). Asset-level risk and return in real estate investments. *The Review of Financial Studies, 34*(8), 3647–3694.

Sandsmark, M., & Vennemo, H. (2007). A portfolio approach to climate investments: CAPM and endogenous risk. *Environmental and Resource Economics, 37*(4), 681–695.

Schied, A. (2007). Optimal investments for risk-and ambiguity-averse preferences: A duality approach. *Finance and Stochastics, 11*(1), 107–129.

Sharp, D. J. (1991). Uncovering the hidden value in high-risk investments. *MIT Sloan Management Review, 32*(4), 69.

Shevchenko, G., Ustinovichius, L., & Andruškevičius, A. (2008). Multi-attribute analysis of investments risk alternatives in construction. *Technological and Economic Development of Economy, 14*(3), 428–443.

Talarico, L., & Reniers, G. (2016). Risk-informed decision making of safety investments by using the disproportion factor. *Process Safety and Environmental Protection, 100*, 117–130.

Thompson, P. B. (1997). Evaluating energy efficiency investments: Accounting for risk in the discounting process. *Energy Policy, 25*(12), 989–996.

Tryhuba, A., Hutsol, T., Tryhuba, I., Pokotylska, N., Kovalenko, N., Tabor, S., & Kwasniewski, D. (2021). Risk assessment of Investments in Projects of production of raw materials for bioethanol. *PRO, 9*(1), 12.

Wang, G., & Wu, R. (2001). Distributions for the risk process with a stochastic return on investments. *Stochastic Processes and their Applications, 95*(2), 329–341.

Weitzman, M. L. (2012). *Rare disasters, tail-hedged investments, and risk-adjusted discount rates* (No. w18496). National Bureau of Economic Research.

2

Time Value of Money

Why is TIME such an important element in your decision?

TIME gives you the opportunity to postpone consumption and earn INTEREST.

For example, 1 euro in hand today is worth more than 1 euro to be received in the future because, if you had it now, you could invest it, earn interest and end up with more than 1 euro in future.

Any amount of money promised in the future is uncertain and riskier than others!

The time value of money principle is concerned with two topics: (1) *future value* and (2) *present value*.

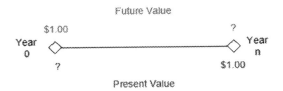

As shown in the illustration above, the two are mirror images of one another. (Year 0 stands for "at the present time" or "right now" since year 1 would be 1 year from now, etc.)

In a *future value* problem, we know the amount of money that we want to invest today (i.e., the present value). What we do not know is how much money we will have in the future (i.e., the future value).

In a *present value* problem, we know the amount of money that we want to have (or expect to have) in the future. What we do not know is how much money we need to invest today to attain that money in the future.

An important tool used in the time value of money analysis is a graphical representation which shows the timing of cash flows.

Moving money through time—that is, finding the equivalent value of money at different points in time—involves translating values from one period to another.

Key Concepts

- Translating a value to the present is referred to as *discounting*.
- Translating a value to the future is referred to as *compounding*.
- Translating money from one period involves *interest*, which is how the time value of money and risk enter the process.

Future Value is the amount to which a cash flow or a series of cash flows will grow over a period when compounded at a given interest rate.

$$FV = PV(1+i)^n$$

- FV = future value or ending amount
- PV = present value or beginning amount
- i = interest rate per period
- n = the number of periods
- $(1 + i)^n$ = future value (interest) factor

2 Time Value of Money

The arithmetic process of determining the final value of a cash flow or series of cash flows when compound interest is applied is called *compounding*.

It is the process of going from today's values or present values (PVs) to future values (FVs), over a period of time (over the timeline).

Present value represents the value today of a future cash flow or a series of cash flows. The present value of a cash flow due n years in the future is the amount which, if it were on hand today, would grow to equal the future amount.

$$PV = \frac{FV}{(1+i)^n}$$

- PV = present value
- FV = future value
- i = interest rate or rate of return
- n = number of periods
- $1/(1 + i)^n$ = present value (interest) factor

Given the formulas above, three questions arise. What happens if the discount periods (n) become larger? But if the interest rate per period (i) becomes larger? What happens with the discount factor and the present value?

Therefore, the *present value* is influenced by both the *interest rate* (i.e., the discount rate) and the *number of discount periods*!

Discounting is the process of finding the present value of a cash flow or a series of cash flows;

Discounting is the reverse of compounding!

Translating a value back in time—referred to as discounting—requires determining *what a future amount or cash flow is worth today.*

Discounting is used in valuation because we often want to determine the value today of some future value or cash flow (e.g., what a bond is worth today if it promised interest and principal repayment in the future).

Interest is the compensation for the opportunity cost of funds and the uncertainty of repayment of the amount borrowed; that is, it represents both the price of time and the price of risk. The *principal* is the amount borrowed. The *price of time* is compensation for the opportunity cost of funds. The *price of risk* is compensation for bearing risk.

There are two types of interests. *Simple interest* and *compound interest*.

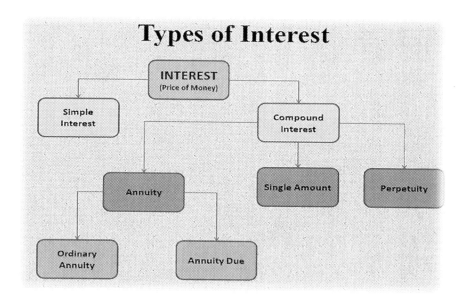

2.1 Simple Interest

Any fund of economic good expressed in monetary form is called *capital*.

A *financial operation* is any action that causes a change in the value of capital.

S_0 is called the initial capital, the initial value, or the current value of the financial operation.

$S_t = S(S_0, t)$ is called the final capital or the final value of the financial operation.

$D = S_t - S_0$ is called the interest corresponding to the capital S_0 for the period t.

Definition We say that a financial operation is carried out in a *simple interest* regime if the interest is calculated on the same capital during its entire use.

Results

- *Final value:* $\boxed{S_t = S_0 + D}$ or $\boxed{S_t = S_0(1 + i \cdot t)}$ (1)

- *Simple Interest:* $\boxed{D = S_0 \cdot i \cdot t}$ (2)
- t is time.
- i it is called the unit annual interest and represents the interest produced by a capital worth 1 m.u. for a period of 1 year.
- $p = 100i$ annual percentage.

If the capital S_0 is placed in simple interest regime with annual percentages $p_1 = 100\ i_1$ during t_1, $p_2 = 100\ i_2$ during t_2, ..., $p_n = 100\ i_n$ during t_n, then the total interest realized during $t = t_1 + t_2 + \ldots + t_n$ is:

$$\boxed{D = S_0\left(i_1 t_1 + i_2 t_2 + \ldots + i_n t_n\right)}\ (3)$$

2.1.1 Solved Problems

1. We make a deposit of a capital $S_0 = 10{,}000$ lei in the simple interest regime for a period of 10 months at a bank that grants the annual percentage of 6%. Determine:

    (a) Interest earned after 10 months.
    (b) The total amount that we will be able to dispose at maturity.

Solution:

It follows that:

- Initial value is: $S_0 = 10{,}000$ lei.
- Duration of the operation is $t = \dfrac{10}{12}$.
- Annual unitary interest is $i = \dfrac{p}{100} = \dfrac{6}{100}$.
  - The interest earned after 10 months is:
  $$D = S_0 \cdot i \cdot t = 10{,}000 \cdot \dfrac{6}{100} \cdot \dfrac{10}{12} = 500 \text{ lei}.$$
  - The amount we will be able to dispose at maturity is:
  $S_t = S_0 + D = 10.500$ lei.

2. What amount must be placed at a simple interest rate for a period of 270 days at a bank that offers an annual percentage of 7% interest to receive 42,100 lei at maturity?

Solution:

We know: Final value St = 42.100, time, expressed in years $t = \dfrac{270}{360}$ and annual interest $i = \dfrac{p}{100} = \dfrac{7}{100}$.

Final value will be: $S_t = S_0(1 + i \cdot t)$ and we get: $S_0 = \dfrac{S_t}{1+it}$,

so $S_0 = \dfrac{42.100}{1 + \dfrac{7}{100} \cdot \dfrac{270}{360}} = 40.000$ lei.

3. How long must a simple interest capital be placed at a bank that grants an annual percentage of 16% interest to withdraw twice the deposited capital at maturity?

Solution:

We know that the final value is:
$S_t = 2S_0$, and the annual interest is $i = \dfrac{16}{100}$.
By plugging the values, we get:

$2S_0 = S_0(1+i \cdot t) \Rightarrow 1+i \cdot t = 2 \Rightarrow t = \dfrac{1}{i} = 6.25$ years, therefore, the amount must be deposited over a period of 6 years and 3 months to double the capital.

4. Starting with January 2020, a person deposits in an account 200 euros on the first day of each month, for 1 year, in simple interest regime, and on the last day of 2020, he liquidates the account. Find out the total interest and the final amount you will have at the liquidation of the account, if the annual percentage is 4% for the entire duration of the operation.

Solution:
We note that 12 deposits are made, with initial values and equal annual percentages,
$S_0 = 200$ euro, $i = \dfrac{p}{100} = \dfrac{4}{100}$ and different placement times:
$t_1 = \dfrac{12}{12}, t_2 = \dfrac{11}{12}, \ldots, t_{12} = \dfrac{1}{12}.$

The total interest realized is given by the sum of the interests produced by each of the 12 amounts placed:

$$D = D_1 + D_2 + \ldots + D_{12} = S_0 i t_1 + S_0 i t_2 + \ldots + S_0 i t_{12}.$$

$$D = S_0 i (t_1 + t_2 + \ldots + t_{12}) = 200 \cdot \dfrac{4}{100} \left(\dfrac{12}{12} + \dfrac{11}{12} + \ldots + \dfrac{1}{12} \right)$$

$$= 200 \cdot \dfrac{4}{100} \cdot \dfrac{78}{12} = 52 \text{ euro.}$$

We got that the total interest is $D = 52$ euros and the final value available for the liquidation of the account is $S_t = 12 S_0 + D = 2,452$ euros.

5. One person opened an account on October 1, 2015, by a deposit in the amount of 60,000 lei in simple interest regime.

Determine what amount will be available on June 30, 2016, if the annual percentage granted by the bank is 8% in October–December 2015, 7% in January–February 2016, and 6% in March–June 2016.

Solution:
The amount we can dispose of when clearing the account is: $S_t = S_0 + D$. We notice that the annual percentage is not constant during the operation.

We calculate the total interest realized, using formula (3) from the theoretical brief:

$$D = S_0\left(i_1 t_1 + i_2 t_2 + i_3 t_3\right) = 60.000\left(\frac{8}{100}\cdot\frac{3}{12} + \frac{7}{100}\cdot\frac{2}{12} + \frac{6}{100}\cdot\frac{4}{12}\right),$$

thus $D = 3.100$ lei.
Therefore, the final value is: $S_t = S_0 + D = 63.100$ lei.

2.1.2 Applications

1. We deposit the amount of 20,000 lei with a simple interest rate for 320 days at a bank that gives the annual percentage rate of 6.5%. Determine the interest and the total amount available at maturity.
2. What amount should be deposited for a trimester in a simple interest rate at a bank that offers the annual percentage 6% for the deposits in lei to be able to raise to the amount of 52,000 lei?
3. At what annual percentage rate an amount of money should be deposited with a simple interest rate at a bank for 2 years so that at maturity we can withdraw double of the amount?
4. For how long do we have to deposit the sum of $400 with simple interest rate with the annual percentage rate 4%, so that at maturity we have 6% more than we deposited?
5. Starting with October 2018, a student deposits 200 lei in an account on the first day of each month, for 10 months, in a simple interest rate, and on July 31, 2019, liquidates the account. Find the total interest and the final value that will be available for the liquidation of the account, if the annual percentage is 7% over the entire duration the operation.

6. A person disclosed his account on September 1, 2018, by a deposit of 12,000 lei with simple interest rate. Determine the amount the person will have, if it liquidates the account on July 30, 2019, if the annual percentage granted by the bank is 7% in the period from September to December 2018, 6.5% in January–February 2019 and 6% in March–July 2019.
7. Starting with the month of January, a person deposits 100 euros on the first day of each month, for 1 year, in a simple interest rate, and on the last day of the year liquidates the account. To find out the total interest and the final value that will be available for the liquidation of the account, knowing that the bank grants to the euro deposits the annual percentage 4% in the first semester of the year and 3% in the second semester.

2.2 Compound Interest

Definition We say that a financial operation is carried out in a *compound interest regime* if the interest is capitalized on each fraction of the duration of the operation.

Specifically, if the duration of the operation is divided into n periods of duration $t_1, t_2, \ldots, t_n$, at the end of each period k, the interest obtained during the period t_k is added to the sum at the beginning of the period and therefore produces interest during the next period $k = \overline{1, n-1}$.

We consider the financial operation of capital placement S_0 for the duration of time t.

We assume that the time duration t is divided into n periods with the durations $t_1, t_2, \ldots, t_n$, and the annual percentages corresponding to these fractions are $p_1 = 100 i_1, p_2 = 100 i_2, \ldots, p_n 100 i_n.$

We denote $S_1, S_2, \ldots, S_n$ the final values of capital S_0 at the end of the n periods.

We apply the formula for calculating the final value in the simple interest regime for each period:

$$S_1 = S_0(1+i_1t_1)$$
$$S_2 = S_1(1+i_2t_2) = S_0(1+i_1t_1)(1+i_2t_2)$$
$$\dots\dots\dots\dots\dots\dots\dots\dots\dots\dots$$
$$S_n = S_{n-1}(1+i_nt_n) = S_0(1+i_1t_1)(1+i_2t_2)\dots(1+i_nt_n).$$

Thus, we get:

$$\boxed{S_n = S_0(1+i_1t_1)(1+i_2t_2)\dots(1+i_nt_n)} \quad (1)$$

Particular Cases

(a) If $t_1 = t_2 = \dots\dots = t_n = 1$ year, then $\boxed{S_n = S_0(1+i_1)(1+i_2)\dots(1+i_n)}$ (2)

(b) If $t_1 = t_2 = \dots\dots = t_m = 1$ year and $i_1 = i_2 = \dots\dots = i_n = i$, then $\boxed{S_n = S_0(1+i)^n}$ (3),

(c) If $t = n + \dfrac{t_m}{m}$ (n years and t_m fractions), then S_t could be calculated:

$$\boxed{S_t = S_0(1+i)^n(1+i_mt_m)} \quad (4) \text{ rational formula}$$

$$\boxed{S_t = S_0(1+i)^{n+\frac{t_m}{m}}} \quad (5) \text{ commercial formula}$$

The compound interest corresponding to the placement of the amount S_0 during period t is:

$$D = S_t - S_0$$

2.2.1 Solved Problems

1. A person who has a capital amount of 10,000 euros may opt for one of the following options for placing it under a compound interest rate for 4 years:

   (a) With a constant annual percentage rate of 4%.
   (b) With the annual percentages 3% in the first year, 4% in the next two and 5% in the last year.

   Determine the final value of the amount placed and the interest obtained in each case.

Solution:

(a) We have: $S_0 = 10.000$ euro; $t = 4$ years, $p = 4\% = > i = 0,04$.

Since the annual percentage is constant throughout the financial operation, we apply formula (3) from the theoretical brief and obtain the final value after 4 years of the amount placed:

$$S_4 = S_0(1+i)^4 = 10.000(1,04)^4 = 11.698,58 \text{ euros.}$$

Hence, the interest is: $D = S_4 - S_0 = 1.698, 58$ euros.

(b) We have: $S_0 = 10.000$ euros; $t = 4$ years; $p_1 = 3\%$, $p_2 = p_3 = 4\%$, $p_4 = 5\% \Rightarrow i_1 = 0.03$, $i_2 = i_3 = 0.04$, $i_4 = 0.05$.

Since the annual percentage is variable, we apply formula (2) from the theoretical brief and obtain the final value after 4 years of the amount placed: $S_4 = S_0(1 + i_1)(1 + i_2)(1 + i_3)(1 + i_4) = 10.000(1,03)(1,04)^2(1,05) = 11.697,50$ euro.

Hence, the interest is: $D = S_4 - S_0 = 1.697,5$ euros.

2. Determine the final amount and interest for a placement of $4000 over 3 years and 5 months, if the annual percentages for the 3 years and 5 months are:

   (a) 5%, 4%, 3.5% and 3% respectively
   (b) 4% for the entire period

Solution:

(a) We have: $S_0 = 4.000\$$; $t = 3 + \dfrac{5}{12}$ years, $i_1 = 0.05$, $i_2 = 0.04$, $i_3 = 0,035$; $i_4 = 0.03$.

Since the annual percentage is variable, we apply formula (2) from the theoretical brief and obtain the final value of the amount placed:

$$S_t = S_0(1+i_1)(1+i_2)(1+i_3)\left(1+i_4 \cdot \dfrac{5}{12}\right) = 4.000(1,05)(1,04)(1,035)\left(1+0,03 \cdot \dfrac{5}{12}\right),$$

thus $S_t = 4.577,39\$$, and the interest is $D = S_t - S_0 = 577,39\ \$$.

(b) We have: $S_0 = 4.000\$$; $t = 3 + \dfrac{5}{12}$ years, $i = 0.04$.

Since the annual percentage is constant and the duration of the operation is not an integer number of years, we can determine the final value using one of the formulas:

* *Rational formula*:

$$S_t = S_0(1+i)^3\left(1+i \cdot \dfrac{5}{12}\right) = 4.000(1,04)^3\left(1+0,04 \cdot \dfrac{5}{12}\right) = 4.574,44\ \$, \text{ so}$$

$$D = S_t - S_0 = 574{,}44\$.$$

- *Commercial formula:*

$$S_t = S_0(1+i)^{3+\frac{5}{12}} = 4.000(1{,}04)^{3+\frac{5}{12}} = 4.506{,}81\ \$,\ and$$

$$D = S_t - S_0 = 506{,}81\$.$$

3. A person will deposit at the beginning of each year, for 4 years, the following amounts: 300, 400, 500, and 600 euros, with the annual percentages corresponding to the 4 years: 5%, 4.5%, 4%, and 3.5%.

   Determine:

   (a) The final value of all deposits at the end of the last investment year.
   (b) What amount should be deposited only once at the beginning of the first year with the mentioned percentages to achieve after 4 years the final value obtained at the point a).

Solution:

(a) We schematically represent the operations that are performed.

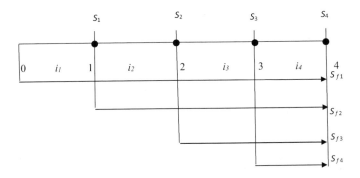

We denote S_{f1}, S_{f2}, S_{f3} and S_{f4} the final values of the four deposits.

The final value of all deposits is given by the sum of the final values of the four deposits:

$$S_f = S_{f1} + S_{f2} + S_{f3} + S_{f4}.$$

As can be seen from the diagram above,

- The final value of the first deposit is determined by applying to the amount S_1 the formula of capitalized for the 4 years: $S_{f1} = S_1(1 + i_1)(1 + i_2)(1 + i_3)(1 + i_4)$.
- The final value of the second deposit is obtained by applying the formula S_2 to the amount capitalized for the second, third, and fourth years: $S_{f2} = S_2(1 + i_2)(1 + i_3)(1 + i_4)$.
- The final value of the third deposit is obtained by applying the formula S3 to the amount S3 fruiting for three and four: $S_{f3} = S_3(1 + i_3)(1 + i_4)$.
- The final value of the fourth deposit is obtained by applying the formula S4 to the amount S_4 capitalized for the second, third, and fourth years: $S_{f4} = S_4(1 + i_4)$.

Thus, the final value of all deposits is:

$$S_f = S_1(1+i_1)(1+i_2)(1+i_3)(1+i_4) + S_2(1+i_2)(1+i_3)(1+i_4) \\ + S_3(1+i_3)(1+i_4) + S_4(1+i_4)$$

$$S_f = (300 \cdot 1.05 \cdot 1.045 \cdot 1.04 \cdot 1.035 + 400 \cdot 1.045 \cdot 1.04 \cdot 1.035 \\ + 500 \cdot 1.04 \cdot 1.035 + 600 \cdot 1.035)$$

$$S_f = 1,963.4591 \text{ lei}.$$

(b) We denote by S_0 the amount to be deposited.

Applying formula (2) from the theory, we have:

$$S_f = S_0(1+i_1)(1+i_2)(1+i_3)(1+i_4) \Rightarrow$$
$$S_0 = \frac{1.963{,}4591}{1.05 \cdot 1.045 \cdot 1.04 \cdot 1.035} = 1{,}662.42 \text{ lei.}$$

4. By what percentage rate must the amount of 10,000 lei be deposited for 3 years under a compound interest regime to be able to achieve an interest in the amount of 4000 lei at maturity?

Solution:
We know: the initial value S_0 = 10, 000 lei, the duration t = 3 years, the interest D = 4000 lei.

Using the formula D = S_t - S_0, we get: S_t = 14, 000 lei.
From the formula that gives the final value, S_t = $S_0(1 + i)^t$, results 14.000 = 10.000 $(1 + i)^3$, thus

$$(1+i)^3 = 1.4 \Rightarrow 1+i = \sqrt[3]{1.4} = 1{,}1186 \Rightarrow i = 0.1186 \Rightarrow p = 11.86\%.$$

5. The following amounts were paid for the purchase of a house: an advance of 10,000 euros and then, in the next 4 years, at the end of each year, the amounts of 3000, 4000, 5000, and 6000 euros. Knowing that the bank used the annual percentage 7%, determine the price at which the house was negotiated.

Solution:
We denote with S_0 initial value and with S_i the payment made at i, $i \in \{2, 3, 4, 5\}$.

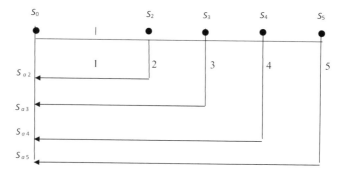

We denote with C the price of the house and with Sa_2, Sa_3, Sa_4 and Sa_5 *actual* values (evaluated at $t = 0$) of the sum S_2, S_3, S_4 and S_5.

The price at with the house was negotiated is given by the sum between the down payment and the present values of the four future payments:

$$C = S_0 + S_{a2} + S_{a3} + S_{a4} + S_{a5}.$$

Thus, as we could see from above,

- The present value of S_2 is determined applying the present value formula for 2 years: $S_{a2} = \dfrac{S_2}{(1+i)^2}$.

- The present value of S_3 is determined applying the present value formula for 3 years: $S_{a3} = \dfrac{S_3}{(1+i)^3}$.

Similarly, we get: $S_{a4} = \dfrac{S_4}{(1+i)^4}$ and $S_{a5} = \dfrac{S_5}{(1+i)^5}$.

Thus, $C = S_0 + \dfrac{S_2}{(1+i)^2} + \dfrac{S_3}{(1+i)^3} + \dfrac{S_4}{(1+i)^4} + \dfrac{S_5}{(1+i)^5}$, i.e.

$$C = 10.000 + \frac{3.000}{1{,}07^2} + \frac{4.000}{1{,}07^3} + \frac{5.000}{1{,}07^4} + \frac{6.000}{1{,}07^5} = 23.977{,}9 \text{ euros}.$$

2.2.2 Applications

1. A person who has a capital of 10,000 euros can opt for one of the following options for placing it in a compound interest rate for 5 years:

    (a) With a constant annual percentage rate 5%
    (b) With annual percentage rates of 4% in the first year, 5% in the next two and 6% in the last 2 years

    Determine the final value of the amount placed and the interest obtained in each case.

2. Determine the final value and the interest related to the placement of the sum of $4000 for 3 years and 9 months, if the annual percentages corresponding to the whole period are:

    (a) 5%, 4%, 2%, and 3% respectively
    (b) 4% for the whole period

3. A person deposits at the beginning of the year, for 4 years, the amounts of 600, 300, 800, and 900 euros respectively, with the annual percentages corresponding to the 4 years: 5%, 4%, 6%, and 7%. Determine:

    (a) The final value of all deposits at the end of the last year of placement.
    (b) What amount should be deposited only once at the beginning of the first year with the mentioned percentages to achieve after 4 years the final value obtained at the point a).

4. At what percentage must be deposited the sum of 1000 lei for 4 years in compound interest regime in order to be able to get at maturity an interest in the value of 600 lei?

5. The following amounts were paid for the purchase of a house: a down payment of 10,000 euros and then the amounts of 4000, 2000, 3000, and 5000 euros in the next 4 years, at the end of each year. Knowing that the bank used the annual percentage 5%, determine the price at which the house was negotiated.
6. You have the amount of 1000,000 lei and place it for 10 years, with an annual percentage of 10% in the first 2 years, 11% in the next 3 and 12% in the last 5 years. Determine the available fund 10 years after the deposit.
7. To make an investment fund, the sum of 4000,000 lei for 10 years, with annual percentages 15% in the first 3 years, 20% in the next 4 years and 25% in the last 3 years. Determine the total fund available after 10 years from now.

3

Financial Markets

The financial market is the mechanism by which financial assets are issued and introduced into the economic circuit. It consists of two major sectors: the banking sector and the financial securities sector.

The movement of funds in the economy can be achieved in two major ways

- Indirect financing: by concentrating cash on hand at banks and their use of the resources attracted for lending to users of funds.
- Direct financing: through the issuance of financial securities by fund users, on the financial market.

The financial market is a generic name to designate the set of relations that are formed, at national level or at international level, between different institutions, legal or natural persons, engaged in the placement and attraction of funds. The financial market consists of several specific markets, whose existence and operation are interconnected both nationally and internationally.

The financial market is at the crossing level of the supply and the demand for funds in the economy and consists of two large segments

- The financial securities market (or the financial market, in a narrow sense) which in turn consists of the money market and the capital market.
- The banking market, i.e., the set of long-term and short-term credit relations, based on non-negotiable assets.

The market for financial securities is one in which financial assets are bought and resold, without changing their nature. In its simplest form, it is a link between holders of surplus funds (investors) and users of funds (issuers of financial securities) and can take two distinct forms: the money market and the capital market.

3.1 Monetary Market

The monetary market includes the relationships that are formed in the field of attracting and placing funds in the short term, usually up to 1 year.

Monetary market operations can take the following forms

- The traditional form of attracting deposits and placing them in the form of loans—as is the case of the interbank market.
- Form of operations with financial assets and short maturities (treasury bills, certificates of deposit, credit securities, etc.).

Each instrument traded on the monetary market has certain characteristics, which leads to the segmentation of the monetary market (the market of certificates of deposit, the market of treasury bills, etc.). The existence of a market for a certain financial instrument implies the existence of a specific mechanism that ensures the "meeting" of the demand with the offer of that type of instrument (Table 3.1).

Financial Securities Trading on the Monetary Market
Characteristics of financial securities traded on the money market:

- They are usually high-value tools.
- They have low risk (some even have zero degree of risk).

Table 3.1 Entities operating in the monetary market

Participants	Main Role
Central Bank	Sells and buys treasury certificates in order to influence the money supply in the economy.
State Treasury	Issue treasury certificates for the population and redeems at maturity and converts treasury certificates into certificates of deposit.
Commercial Banks	They trade various short-term financial securities as part of their management treasury.
Companies, firms	Trade in government securities, treasury bills, certificates of deposit in your own name and for clients, grant and receive loans and term loans.
Investment companies (brokerage firms)	Trade financial instruments on behalf of their customers
Financing companies (leasing)	Lend funds to individuals
Insurance companies	It provides its liquidity needs in order to meet unexpected demands.
Pension funds	Places funds in money market instruments (along with investments in stocks and bonds)
Individuals	Occasionally buy money market instruments and units of money market funds.
Money market funds	Facilitates the participation of small investors in the market by aggregating their funds and placing them in large value instruments.

- They have a maturity of 1 year or even less from the date of issue. For most instruments traded on the money market, the maturity is less than 120 days.

Treasury bills/treasury certificates are securities issued by the monetary authorities of different countries and put up for sale to attract short-term funds available from banks, firms, and individuals for the temporary coverage of budgetary and government expenditures. The main feature of treasury bills is that they are guaranteed by the state, thus being considered "risk-free."

Treasury bills are issued according to a certain schedule (usually new issues replacing those that have matured) and have maturities of 1, 3, 6, or 12 months, with different nominal values, but there is a minimum level established by custom. Being bearer securities, the treasury bills are easily traded, having a high degree of liquidity, they represent, in essence, a payment commitment, at maturity, assumed by the state.

There are treasury bills that are sold to different investors at the issue, at a price lower than the nominal value of the document, and at maturity the investor receives the nominal value of the security. Thus, the profit of the financial investment results from the difference between the purchase price (lower) and the price received at maturity (higher). In this context, one can discuss an implicit interest rate, or, in other words, the efficiency of the operation.

The issuance mechanism of these securities is the auction, being sold to those investors who for a given amount of treasury bills offer the best price (of course, below face value).

They can be offered to the public directly through the state treasury departments (the ministry of finance, for example) or, in some cases, the central bank is also involved in this process.

The default interest rate (yield) is calculated based on the issue price and not based on the face value of the treasury bill. The formula for calculating the yield (R) is:

$$R = \frac{P_r - P_e}{P_e} \times \frac{360}{n} \times 100$$

where,

- P_e—the issue price.
- P_r—redemption price.
- n—the number of days for which the title is held.

If the security changes ownership until maturity, a return on the investment of each new holder may be determined, considering the purchase price, the sale price, and the number of days for which the instrument is held:

$$R = \frac{P_v - P_a}{P_a} \times \frac{360}{n} \times 100$$

where,

- P_v—selling price.
- P_a—purchase price.
- n—the number of days for which the title is held.

As the issuance of treasury bills has a relatively regular character, with standardized procedures and public institutions involved, within the money market, the treasury bill market is the most active and highly liquid segment.

The Certificate of Deposit (CD) is a negotiable document that confirms the deposit of funds denominated in a certain currency, for a short period of time, usually 3 months.

Certificates of deposit are issued by commercial banks or other institutions that attract deposits. Like treasury bills, certificates of deposit are bearer financial securities and interest is implicit, resulting from the difference between the purchase price at issue and the redemption price at maturity.

Although guaranteed by the issuing institution, these securities are considered riskier than treasury bills, which makes them less "liquid." Therefore, the (default) interest rate for CDs must be higher to reward the investor for the increased risk of default or market. Thus, at the yield level, there is a difference that has the characteristics of a risk premium. Of course, the size of the risk premium depends on the credit worthiness of the issuing institution.

Certificates of deposit can be placed to investors either directly or through brokers and institutions specializing in their placement. In the case of certificates of deposit, the issuance mechanism is not the auction, but the negotiation between the parties.

The yield on a certificate of deposit is calculated in the same way as for a treasury bill.

Trade effects are financial securities issued by financial institutions and companies as a way of financing the need for short-term liquidity. Generally, the maturity of these securities is from 1 month to 3 months.

Specific Features

- They are instruments not explicitly guaranteed by the issuer.
- They can only be resold in certain situations.

Like certificates of deposit, bills of exchange are issued in three ways

- Direct placement.
- Through a specialized placement agency.
- Through a department of the issuer, specialized in investments (preferred variant by financial institutions that regularly issue trade bills to finance their activity).

Obviously, the issuer's reputation is particularly important for the success of the show. Therefore, many issuing companies use rating agencies to classify issues, although they are considered a good ranking as not always a guarantee against risk. Therefore, most experienced investors appreciate that the rating is only an indicator in the investment process and an element to be considered in the decision to place commercially available funds.

Investors in commercial securities are often large non-bank financial institutions—such as insurance companies or mutual funds, which in this way place funds in the short term. In the case of mature money markets, the trade effects market is often an alternative to other segments of the money market (certificates of deposit or treasury bills for the placement of available funds).

The yield of trade effects is higher than in the case of certificates of deposit. The calculation method is similar to that presented for the tools described above. From the point of view of the issuer, if he appeals for the placement of the documents to the services of a specialized intermediary, he must deduct from the sale price of the securities the commission of the placement agency.

Medium-Term Trade Effects

Although, typically, the bills have a maturity of up to 3 months, such securities with a maturity of 6 or 12 months may be issued. In this situation, their sale will be made by individual investors. Trading securities with a maturity of up to 5 years can only be sold to institutional investors and are called medium-term securities.

The repurchase agreement (repo) is an agreement between two money market participants regarding the temporary sale of securities, with the obligation to be repurchased at a date and at a specified price, at the conclusion of the agreement. In general, the maturity of the operation can be from 1 day to 2–3 weeks; less often, repo contracts with maturities of more than 30 days can be encountered. The redemption price is higher than the sale price, the difference representing the investor's profit (in the form of an implicit interest).

In fact, a repo contract is a loan secured by financial assets. The investor lends a sum of money to the holder of the assets and temporarily takes possession of the property right over the respective financial assets. Thus, financial securities, in fact, represent the guarantee for credit. If the debtor does not repurchase the assets at the agreed maturity, the investor has the right to resell them to recover the amounts advanced.

The reverse repo contract is the repo contract viewed from the investor's perspective. Due to the low risk, government securities are the most used assets in repo contracts. However, certificates of deposit or bills of exchange can also be found. Repo contracts are a way of using financial assets for short-term financing when their holder does not want to sell them permanently from his portfolio. Thus, a repo contract is a way in which financial institutions use financial assets to manage very short-term liquidity, in parallel with keeping them in the portfolio as long-term investments.

And in the case of repo contracts, the yield is calculated according to the formula presented above.

The bill of exchange is a very common credit used in international trade relations. In brief, the bill of exchange is a document by which a person (drawer) orders another person (drawn) to make a payment at a certain maturity to a third person (beneficiary). Usually, the issuance of the bill of exchange is based on a commercial transaction.

The seller, the issuer of the bill of exchange (drawer), in order to have the security of collecting the equivalent value of the bill of exchange at maturity, asks the buyer (drawer) to accept it by himself or by a bank (bank acceptance). If the acceptance is given by the buyer, the bank guarantee is also guaranteed by the bank. In this way, the bill of exchange becomes a security that gives the holder the certainty that at maturity he will collect the money by bank acceptance or endorsement. In other words, if the buyer does not pay at maturity, the bank will honor the payment obligation.

The buyer of the goods pays the bank a commission for this service, the bank being able to request a guarantee in the event that the importer will not make the payment at the due date stipulated in the bill of exchange.

The seller in possession of the bill of exchange may wait for the maturity to receive payment or, to obtain liquidity, may resort to discounting the bill of exchange or sell the security before maturity to commercial banks. By discounting, the holder of the title obtains its nominal value minus the interest (discount) for the amount received, calculated from the moment of discounting until the due date. Thus, the discount appears as a loan given by the commercial bank to the holder of the credit title, on the interval between the two moments. Bills of exchange are securities guaranteed by banks, and ownership of them can be easily transferred by pledge or endorsement.

3.2 Capital Market

The capital market represents the set of relations and mechanisms through which the transfer of funds from those who have a capital surplus—investors—to those who need capital, with the help of specific instruments (issued securities) and through specific operators (securities companies).

Unlike the monetary market, the capital market specializes in conducting transactions with financial assets with medium and long maturities. Through it, available capital is channeled to national or international economic operators, where capital needs exceed domestic financial coverage possibilities or monetary authorities impose certain restrictions on access to domestic financial resources.

The diversity of traded products, of the procedures and techniques of sale-purchase of financial securities as well as of the different ways of finalizing the transactions or the way of forming the price of securities imposed the structuring of the capital market in relation to different criteria, as follows:

1. From the point of view of the production and marketing of financial securities, the capital market comprises two segments:
   (a) The primary market is the market through which new issues of financial instruments are traded for the first time.
   (b) The secondary market is the market on which instruments already in circulation are traded. The secondary market provides liquidity for investors who want to change their portfolios before the maturity date.

2. According to the object of the transaction, the following are different:
   (a) The stock market
   (b) The bond market
   (c) Forward contracts market (forward and futures)
   (d) Options market

3. According to the model of forming the price of financial securities, the capital market is structured in:
   (a) The auction market is the market in which trading is conducted by a third party based on the overlap of prices on orders received to buy or sell a certain security. The trader is an agent for financial investment services. Demands and offers mention both the price and the quantity to be traded. Transactions are made at those prices for which there is both demand and supply. Buyers and sellers do not trade directly and generally do not know the identity of the other party. The market is impersonal and organized, operating according to well-established trading rules.

(b) The negotiation market is the market in which buyers and sellers negotiate between themselves the price and the volume of real estate either directly or through intermediaries. If the transaction is carried out through an intermediary, the identity of one of the parties may or may not be known to the other party. Negotiation takes time to identify buyers and sellers and to review the price or volume to be traded.

4. Depending on the time of completion of transactions are different:
    (a) The spot market or the cash market on which the securities are traded for immediate delivery and payment. "Immediate" is defined by that market and varies from 1 day to 1 week depending on the regulations in force.
    (b) The forward market is the market in which the completion of transactions related to the delivery of securities to the new buyer and the payment is made at a future date. In this market, transactions take place on a firm term, when there is certainty of their completion at a certain maturity and on a conditional term, when the finality depends on the future evolution of the exchange rate and is left to the buyer who bears a cost for the right to cancel. Contract.

The capital market ensures the permanent connection between issuers and investors both at the moment of covering the capital demand and in the process of transforming the held financial securities into liquidity. As mentioned above, viewed in terms of the procedure and trading of financial securities, the capital market consists of two major components: the primary market and the secondary market.

The primary market is the one on which newly issued securities are sold and bought (for example, when a company issue shares when setting up or increasing the share capital). This market ensures the meeting between the demand and the supply of securities, allowing the financing of the activity of the companies. It is therefore a means of distributing securities by users of funds and investing in securities by holders of funds.

The primary market is a specialized financing circuit. This market allows the direct transformation of economies into long-term resources, as well as the financing of companies.

The participants in the primary market are:

- Title providers (this category may include the state and local authorities, public and private enterprises).
- Capital providers (private individuals, enterprises, banks, and insurance companies).
- Intermediaries (there are service companies, financial investment companies, commercial banks, investment companies that ensure the sale of financial securities through their own network).

The primary market is also called the issue market. The issue of financial securities can be done through bidding (competitive), direct negotiation between the parties involved (issuers of securities and investors) or with the help of intermediaries. Generally, the issue is subscribed by intermediaries to guarantee the subsequent sale of all securities issued. Therefore, on the primary market are sold the financial securities issued by those entities that need financial resources (securities providers) and are bought by other entities or individuals with medium- and long-term savings (capital providers).

The secondary market is the market on which financial securities are traded after issuance. This market fulfills, like the primary one, a role of concentration of the demand and supply of securities, but of a derivative demand and supply, which manifests itself after the securities market has been established. As a rule, those who subscribe to guarantee the issue do not keep their purchased securities, but in turn, either directly or through specialized intermediaries, sell them on the secondary market.

The secondary market ensures through the stock exchange both the proper functioning of the primary market and the liquidity and mobility of capital. Investors could sell their financial securities held in the portfolio at any time or they can buy new ones.

The secondary market concentrates the demand and the derived supply that manifests itself after the market of financial securities has been constituted. Thus, the secondary market is essential for the success of the issues made on the primary market because it offers the buyer the possibility to convert his acquired securities into money at any time, by selling them to other investors.

The secondary market is an organized market that provides operators with the following advantages:

1. Provides information regarding the security to be traded.
2. The information about the security and the issuer is transmitted to the large mass of investors.
3. Provides information on the level and movement of the market price.
   The objectives of the secondary market are:

   (a) Investor protection achieved through transparency, regulation, and market surveillance.
   (b) Market liquidity and exchange rate stability.

An important role on the capital market belongs to the intermediaries who assume the commitment to distribute the securities issued on the primary market, facilitate the trade with them, respectively the sale-purchase of financial securities both in their own name and on their own account and on behalf of third parties.

Intermediaries may specialize in one or more activities. Some act primarily on the primary market by ensuring the distribution and placement of new issues, while others act only on the secondary market, the latter being represented by brokerage firms or dealers.

The two market segments are inter-conditioned. The secondary market cannot exist without the primary position and at the same time the functioning of the primary market is influenced by the capacity of the secondary market to achieve the transferability of financial securities and their transformation into liquidity.

Advantages and disadvantages of financing a company by issuing shares

Advantages	Disadvantages
Reputation—the fact that the company is listed, together with the high level of transparency of information, determines the achievement of a better ranking and an improved public image of the company.	Obligation to *publish certain information*—listed companies must make public certain information about their activity. This is an additional task for driving and increases the costs.
Financial flexibility—access to capital markets means that listed companies can have increased flexibility in how to structure their capital.	*Reduced flexibility to change*—the company's policies must be in line with investors' forecasts. Consequently, there are fewer opportunities to change the company's strategy.
Development opportunities—the possibility to offer actions, as a way of payment based on the purchases made, implies that there are increased development opportunities through by this method.	*Takeover risk*—the risk that the majority stake will be acquired through a hostile takeover becomes a reality.
Transforming the investment into liquid funds—the existence of a liquid secondary market means that owners/shareholders can sell their shares in a very short time, recovering his investment.	*Trading* based on internal information—this problem is associated with the use of information confidentiality that influences the share price.

3.2.1 Instruments Presented on the Capital Market

The asset represents a good belonging to a person, and which can be capitalized in the economic activity. Depending on the nature of the capitalization process, assets can be of two types: real and financial. Real assets are represented by tangible or intangible assets which, integrated in the economic circuit, generate income in the future in the form of profits, rents, rents, etc. The financial assets are materialized in documents (papers or records in the account), which enshrine the money rights of their holder, as well as his rights over income from the capitalization of those assets (interest, dividends, etc.).

Financial assets represent the monetary correspondent of real assets, and they reveal the dual character of the market economy: real economy, respectively material processes of production of goods and services necessary for individual consumption or production, and symbolic or financial economy, i.e., information processes, represented by the movement of money and securities.

Accordingly, capital, in the sense of an asset that is capitalized over time, can be seen in the form of real capital and financial capital. The financial counterfeit of real capital, financial assets, represented by money and a multitude of securities (bills of exchange, treasury bills, shares, bonds, etc.), play an important role in the general movement of capital in the modern economy. As a financial form of real assets, financial assets ensure the regulation of economic life, the reproduction of real, productive capital, while also tending to capitalize autonomously.

As already mentioned, on the capital market, the money circuit—the "lubricant of economic life"—is made between those who provide funds and those who use them. Basically, this means the issuance of financial assets by fund users and their distribution to fund holders.

Financial assets can be classified into two broad categories

* Banking assets–are the assets resulting from the specific operations of banks and similar institutions. Characteristic of these assets is the fact that they produce interest, are non-negotiable and have a high degree of security.
* Non-banking financial assets—are the assets resulting from investment operations (investment) and which are materialized in negotiable financial securities. This category includes both capital assets—resulting from long-term investments that give the right to obtain future income—and monetary assets—resulting from short-term investments and negotiable on the money market.

Financial securities represent the way non-banking assets exist, these being securities that give their holders the right to obtain, under specified conditions, a part of the future income of the issuer.

All financial securities that are the subject of transactions on the capital market are also called stock products. From the point of view of the way they are created, they fall into three main categories: primary, derivative, and synthetic.

Primary securities (or restricted financial securities) are those issued by users of equity capital funds—also called equity instruments—and those used to attract loan capital—also called debt instruments. Debt instruments). The first category includes shares, and the second includes bonds. The defining characteristic of primary securities is that they, on the one hand, ensure the long-term capital mobilization by users of funds, and on the other hand, give their holders rights over those net income to the issuer, the investor being thus directly associated to the profit and risk of the fund user's business.

Derivative securities are stock exchange products resulting from contracts concluded between the issuer (seller) and the beneficiary (buyer) and which give the latter rights over some assets of the issuer at a certain future maturity, under the conditions established in the contract.

Unlike primary securities, they do not carry rights over the issuer's net monetary income, but over various assets, such as financial securities, currencies, commodities, etc. At the same time, because the existence and market value of these securities depend on the assets to which they refer, they are called derivative securities. These derivative securities fall into two categories: futures and options.

Synthetic securities result from the combination of different financial assets by financial companies and the creation of a new investment instrument on this basis. Synthetic products can be made by combining futures contracts of sale and purchase, put and call options, as well as by combinations between different types of futures and options.

A special category of synthetic assets is represented by "basket securities," which are based on a selection of primary financial securities, combined to result in a standardized stock product. The best-known securities of this kind are stock index contracts.

Capital Market Operations

Diversification of investments, placement of available amounts in several different savings and investment instruments, and/or in different variants of the same type of instrument (in several different shares listed on the stock exchange or in securities in several mutual funds), has an important role in substantiating the investment decision.

We must pursue that type of investment that ensures an optimal ratio between profitability and risk, a ratio adjusted according to expectations, possibilities and finally the risk aversion of each investor.

There are many types of investments available to a savings holder. Most can fall into the following categories: amounts held in national currency (lei); amounts held in convertible currencies; certificates of deposit, deposits, or amounts held with commercial banks, CECs, or other financial institutions; government securities; participation titles in investment funds; shares and bonds of public companies, listed on the stock exchange market; futures investments (futures and options contracts); other ways of investing, such as insurance policies (life insurance) and other instruments of insurance companies; direct investments in unlisted companies real estate investments; alternative investments (gold, antiques, works of art).

In most cases, the main market is the stock market, which means that all transactions are made through the central system of the stock exchange, and securities prices are listed continuously.

3.2.2 Solved Problems

1. An investor purchases a treasury bill, with the maturity at 6 months and a nominal value of 200 thousand m.u., at a price of 180 thousand m.u. What is the yield of this instrument if it is held to maturity and repurchased by investors at face value?

$$R = \frac{200-180}{180} \times \frac{360}{180} \times 100 = 22.22\%$$

2. An investor purchases a stock for 12.45 lei and is selling it after 3 quarters for 14.25 lei. What is the return of the investment?

$$R = \frac{14.25-12.45}{12.45} \times \frac{360}{270} \times 100 = 19.27\%$$

3. Calculate the yield for the following treasury bills with a face value of 100 mil. Lei.

   (a) An instrument with a maturity of 60 days is purchased with 90 mil lei.
   (b) An instrument with a maturity of 4 months is purchased 40 days before maturity at a price of 95 mil lei.
   (c) The treasury bill from the above situation (part b) is sold after 30 days with 97 million lei. Calculate the yield of the sellers.

$$R = \frac{100-90}{90} \times \frac{360}{60} \times 100 = 66.67\%$$

$$R = \frac{100-95}{95} \times \frac{360}{40} \times 100 = 47.36\%$$

$$R = \frac{97-95}{95} \times \frac{360}{30} \times 100 = 25.26\%.$$

4. Calculate the yield of a certificate of deposit of 1000 lei with a maturity of 10 days, which is sold for 990 lei.

$$R = \frac{1000-990}{990} \times \frac{360}{10} \times 100 = 36.36\%$$

3.2.3 Applications

1. Calculate the yield of a certificate of deposit of 540 USD with a maturity of 90 days, which is sold for 480 USD.
2. A company issues trading effects with a maturity of 60 days, with a redemption value of 100 million euros. These are placed through a trading company that charges a commission of 4% of the value of the trade effects. The amount obtained by the issuer, before deducting the placement commission, is 90 million euros. What is the efficiency of the operation for the buyer? But for the issuer?

3. An enterprise issues 90-day trading effects with a redemption value of 90 thousand USD. These are placed through an investment company that charges a commission of 5% of the value of the trade effects. The amount obtained by the issuer, before deducting the placement commission, is 80 thousand USD. What is the efficiency of the operation for the buyer? But for the issuer?
4. An investor purchases a stock for 2.45 USD and selling it after one semester for 2.53 USD. What is the return of the investment? What is the return of the investment, given that the investor received a dividend of 0.5 USD?
5. An investor purchases a stock for 3.51 euro and is selling it after 120 days for 3.42 euro. What is the return of the investment, given that the investor received no dividend? What is the return of the investment, given that the investor received a dividend of 1 euro?
6. A company issues trading effects with a maturity of 60 days, with a redemption value of 100 million euros. These are placed through an investment company that charges a commission of 2.5% of the value of the trade effects. The amount obtained by the issuer, before deducting the placement commission, is 98 million euros. What is the efficiency of the operation for the buyer? But for the issuer?
7. A company issues trading effects with a maturity of 120 days, with a redemption value of 80 million USD. These are placed through a specialized company that charges a commission of 1.5% of the value of the trade effects. The amount obtained by the issuer, before deducting the placement commission, is 72.4 million USD. What is the efficiency of the operation for the buyer? But for the issuer?
8. An investor purchases a stock for 1.01 euro and is selling it after 240 days for 1.01 euro.

    (a) What is the return of the investment, given that the investor received no dividend?
    (b) What is the return of the investment, given that the investor received a dividend of 0.1 euro?

9. Calculate the yield of a certificate of deposit of 1240 m.u. with a maturity of 100 days, which is sold for 1140 m.u. Find the return.

10. Calculate the yield for the following treasury bills with a face value of 100 million lei.

    (a) An instrument with a maturity of 50 days is purchased with 80 mil lei.
    (b) An instrument with a maturity of 7 months is purchased 1 month before maturity at a price of 96 mil lei.
    (c) The treasury bill from the above situation is sold after 20 days with 97 million lei.

    - Calculate the yield of the sellers (20 days).
    - Calculate the yield of the buyer (10 days).

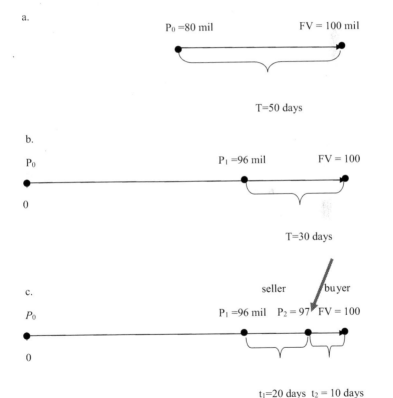

11. Find the financial value of a share given that a dividend of $2.24 paid by a company, given that the average market interest rate was 6.25%.
12. Find the yield value of a stock of a company in 2018, given that the net profit distributed per share was 23.45 lei, while the average market interest rate in the previous year was 4.23%.
13. Find the issue price of a stock, given that the nominal value is 5.24 m.u. and the issue premium was 1.17 m.u.
14. Calculate the yield for the following treasury bills with a face value of 1000 euro.

    (a) An instrument with a maturity of 3 months is purchased with 700 euro.
    (b) An instrument with a maturity of 4 months is purchased 3 months before maturity at a price of 800 euro.
    (c) The treasury bill from the above situation is sold after 1 month with 950-euro.

    - Calculate the yield of the sellers.
    - Calculate the yield of the buyer.

Useful formulas:

- $$R = \frac{P_r - P_e}{P_e} \times \frac{360}{n} \times 100$$

    P_e—purchasing value.
    P_r—face value;
    n—number of days.

- $$R = \frac{P_v - P_a}{P_a} \times \frac{360}{n} \times 100$$

    P_v—selling value;
    P_a—purchasing value;
    n—number of days.

- $R_{issuer} = \dfrac{P_v - (P_a - c\% \cdot P_a)}{P_a - c\% \cdot P_a} \times \dfrac{360}{n} \times 100$

- $R_{buyer} = \dfrac{P_v - (P_a)}{P_a} \times \dfrac{360}{n} \times 100$

P_v—selling value;
P_a—purchasing value;
n—number of days.
c—commission

- $R = \dfrac{P_r - P_e + D}{P_e} \times \dfrac{360}{n} \times 100$

P_e—purchasing value;
P_r—face value;
n—number of days.
D—dividend.

4

Stock Market

Shares are securities that certify a right of ownership over a part of the share capital of the issuing company. Basically, the owner of the shares is the owner of a part of the issuing company, part corresponding to the number of shares held. In addition to the ownership of a part of the issuing company, the shares also confer other rights, the most important of which are:

- The right to receive each year a share of the company's profit (in the form of dividends) corresponding to the number of shares held and the amount allocated by the company's management for the payment of dividends. Due to the fact that this dividend can vary (or can even be zero), the shares are also called variable income securities.
- The right to information on the economic and financial evolution of the enterprise.
- The right to participate in important decisions regarding the company's activity, as well as to the company's management, by participating in the General Meetings of Shareholders (GMS), respectively by the possibility to elect and be elected in the company's board of directors.
- Property right over a part of the company's assets, in case of its liquidation (cessation of operation), etc.

Currently, the shares of listed Romanian companies are traded on two organized markets: the Bucharest Stock Exchange and the Rasdaq stock exchange company.

The action is a financial security that allows you to finance your business. Actions can allow the mobilization of share capital, ensuring its formation and, possibly, its increase.

Classification of Shares

Several types of shares are issued and traded on the stock market, which can be classified according to the form of presentation and the rights they generate.

According to the presentation form, there are registered shares and bearer shares.

Registered shares—are personalized by mentioning the name of their holder who have a restrictive circulation, in the sense that they can be alienated only by transcribing the transaction in the register of the issuing company. The registered shares can be:

* Registered names, in which case the shares are registered simultaneously in the company's register and in the account of the financial intermediary chosen by their owner to whom the purchase and sale orders are sent.
* Pure names—which are registered only in the register of the company that ensures the free management of the securities. Without exception, this formula attracts administrative formalities (entails costs and delays) when reselling securities: they must first be converted into bearer shares or, if the company's articles of association do not allow, into registered shares.

Bearer shares—are shares whose movement is free, their owner benefiting from all the rights and obligations arising from their holding. The securities are called bearer when the issuing company does not know their owner. The simple entry in the register made by the intermediary responsible for the owner's account is sufficient to prove the ownership of the title. These securities can be traded without term and without formalities. The movements of the securities are materialized in simple accounting documents between intermediaries (that of the buyer and that of the seller).

Depending on the rights they generate, the shares can be ordinary, preferred, or preferential.

The most common are simple (ordinary) actions, in fact the only ones allowed in Romania. They give the holder the right to vote, to annual dividends—the size of which is directly proportional to the ratio between the value of the shares and the profit distributed to shareholders, as well as a proportional part of the capital surplus, after paying debts, when the company enters liquidation.

The preferred shares entitle the shareholders to a fixed dividend, regardless of the size of the company's profit.

The preferential shares do not give the shareholder the right to vote in the general meeting, but they have priority when receiving pre-established dividends either in absolute value or in relative value. Preferential actions can be

- Cumulative, whose unpaid dividends due to the inefficiency of the company are accumulated. They shall be paid before any other dividends intended for the common shares at the time the profit is distributed.
- Non-cumulative, whose unpaid dividends due to insufficient economic results cannot be accumulated in favor of the shareholder.
- Participating companies, which, in addition to the pre-issue dividend, also receive a certain percentage of the dividend intended for common shares. This type of share comprises two categories of dividends: a dividend predetermined by a clause and a participation dividend, the actual amount of which is determined once the dividend of the common shares has been calculated.
- Non-participants, who receive a fixed dividend predetermined at issue.
- With variable dividend—are those whose dividends expressed as a percentage are adjusted according to current interest rate variations.
- Priority—are those actions whose payment is made before all preferential actions.
- Convertibles, which at the request of the holder can be transformed into common shares.

- Revocable—are the shares for which the issuer reserves the right to redeem them from the market at a predetermined price.
- Investment certificates—results from the division of a common share into a voting certificate and an investment certificate. The latter confers the right to the same dividend as the joint stock from which it originates. As for the voting certificate, it is assigned to former shareholders who subscribe or not to an investment certificate. An investment certificate is a voting certificate held by the same holder without necessarily being reconstituted in a share.

4.1 Value and Price of the Stocks

The circulation of shares through sale-purchase on a specific market is made free through the mechanism of supply and demand, forming a price called exchange rate, which may be different from the nominal price recorded per share. The variations of the exchange rate are determined by the economic-financial results of the issuing company, by the conjunctural economic climate, by the ratio between the demand and the offer of shares, etc.

To increase its capital, an enterprise can

- To incorporate in its capital the benefits it has accumulated in the form of reserves which, being the property of the shareholders, allow the issuance, in their favor, of free shares. The shareholders benefit, in this case, depending on the number of securities held, from a negotiable allotment right, which allows the shareholders who do not possess the exact number of securities necessary to benefit from the allotment, to buy or sell rights.

Example
A share is worth 24 euros. It was decided to award one new free share for five old shares. Instead of having five shares worth 120 euros, the shareholder will have six shares also worth theoretically 120 euros because overall, the company's own funds have not changed. 20 euros per share. The difference between the course of the action before and after the

award, 4 euros, represents the theoretical value of the award right. As, for the subscription right, the award right is quoted on the market and its exchange rate is not necessarily equal to its theoretical value, the award should not be confused with the division of shares which consists in the division of the nominal value of a share giving rise to several shares. For example, splitting the par value of a 10 euro share into two will result in two shares with a par value of 5 euro. The stock exchange price of the shares will also be divided into two. Its purpose is to facilitate exchanges.

* To request new capital to finance investments and to issue cash shares in return. Except for those who resign, shareholders will enjoy a preferential subscription right to this capital increase. So, in the case of the subscription right, a company makes a public call for savings to increase its revenues. In this case, it will first call on its own shareholders to allow them, if they wish, to maintain their shareholding. This subscription right is negotiable on the stock exchange. (This right may not be exercised if the shareholders waive it at an extraordinary general meeting). The right period is the time interval in which the old shareholders can subscribe, and the right period—the interval in which the new shareholders can subscribe.

Example
The capital of a company comprises two million shares. A capital increase provides for the issuance of 500.00 new shares, i.e., a new share for four old ones. The new shares are issued at a price of 20 euros, while the share price on the stock exchange for the old shares (before issue) is 22 euros. The owner of four shares at 22 euros can buy an extra one at 20 euros. His portfolio is now 108 euros for five shares, which is 21.6 euros per share, the share price after the issue. The difference between the share price before and after, of 0.4 euros, represents the theoretical value of the subscription right. This right, being quoted during the period of capital increase, its exchange rate may evolve depending on the market's expectations on the share price.

As a means of investment, the share is characterized by a certain value, which is considered under the following aspects:

(a) The nominal value is a conventional value, based on which the capital is divided between the shareholders. Shares may not be issued for an amount less than the nominal value. The nominal value of a share cannot be less than 0.10 lei. Depending on this value, a basic remuneration of the shareholders is provided by the statute.

Nominal value (NV) equal to the amount of share capital (SC) divided by the number of shares issued (*N*):

$$NV = \frac{CS}{N}$$

(b) The patrimonial value—expressed by the book value and the intrinsic value.

The book value expresses the part of the net asset that belongs to a share, respectively, the net (accounting) asset that belongs to the holder of a share.

$$V_{ct} = \frac{An}{N}$$

- V_{ct}—book value
- An—net assets (equity)
- N—total number of shares

The net assets are represented by the part of the company's assets not affected by the debts contracted by it.

$$An = At - Dt$$

- An—net assets
- At—total assets (real)
- Dt—total debts

The *intrinsic value* expresses the net asset adjusted by the pluses or minuses of latent assets that return on a share. Latent assets are provisions for risks and expenses that did not arise in the year ended and that did not result in income statements.

$$VI = \frac{Anc}{N}$$

Where,

- VI—intrinsic value.
- Anc—corrected net assets.
- N—the total number of shares issued and in circulation.

Intrinsic value is also the result of the ratio between equity and the number of shares outstanding.

$$VI = \frac{CP}{N} = \frac{CS + Rl}{N}$$

- CP—equity
- CS—share capital
- Rl—legal reserves constituted by the issuer
- N—number of shares issued and in circulation

The intrinsic value is not an immediately usable value. In the event of the liquidation of the issuing company, a shareholder's right to the issuer's assets is equal to the intrinsic value.

(c) Profitability value, interpreted as financial value and yield value.

The *financial value* expresses the financial capital that would be obtained through a dividend comparable to the average market interest rate:

$$Vf = \frac{D}{Rmd}$$

- Vf—financial value
- D—the dividend
- Rmd—average market interest rate

The *return value* is considered a form of expression of the financial value, being calculated as the ratio between the distributed net profit per share and the average market interest rate.

$$Vr = \frac{Pna}{Rmd}$$

- Vr—yield value
- Pna—net profit per share
- Rmd—average market interest rate

The sale of shares at the time of issue or at any time on the capital market is carried out at the issue price or at the market price. This is how they differ

(d) Negotiated value or issue price, which is determined by adding to the face value of the issue premium:

$$PE = VN + pe$$

- PE—issue price
- VN—face value
- Pe—the issue premium

The sale of the shares at the issue price provides the issuer with an additional contribution to the capital.

(e) The *market value*, respectively, the price at which the share transactions are performed. This value is in the form of a stock exchange rate.

For a capital market investor, the investment decision is influenced by the information he can obtain regarding the valuation of shares at a given time. For this purpose, the financial evaluation of the actions and their technical evaluation shall be carried out.

4.2 Stock Valuation

The fundamental evaluation (also called financial evaluation) is performed on the basis of financial indicators, of which the most used are presented below.

(a) *Earnings per share*—expresses the issuer's ability to make a profit and is calculated using the relation:

$$\text{PPA} = \frac{\text{PN}}{N}$$

- PPA—profit per share;
- PN—net profit;
- N—the total number of existing shares on the market.

(b) *Dividend distribution rate*—reflects the part of the profit for the financial year distributed to shareholders.

$$d = \frac{D_n}{P_n} \times 100$$

- d—dividend distribution rate;
- D_n—net dividends (calculated after paying the dividend tax)
- P_n—net profit

The size of this indicator depends on the decision on profit distribution, namely:

- If "d" tends to zero, the issuer's concern for ensuring self-financing by reinvesting profit results.
- If "d" tends to 100%, there is a concern to maintain the interest of shareholders to hold the shares of the company that distributes large dividends.
- If "d" is equal to 100%, the issuing company does not incorporate in the reserve any monetary unit from the profit obtained.
- If "d" is greater than 100%, the previously accumulated reserves are used in order to distribute them as dividends.

(c) Dividend per share, calculated both as gross dividend distributed and as net dividend:

$$\text{DPA} = \frac{\text{Pnr}}{N}$$

- DPA—dividend per share
- Pnr—net profit distributed to shareholders
- N—the total number of existing shares on the market

The dividend per share represents, for the owner of the share, the income produced by his investment, so it is a financial flow. In contrast, earnings per share are an important element of the valuation of a share for the issuer.

(d) *Yield of a share*—is produced both by dividends and by the increase of the market value of the share.

$$R = \frac{D + C_1 - C_0}{C_0} \times 100$$

- *R*—yield of an action
- *D*—the dividend distributed
- C_1—the course for resale of the share
- C_0—the price of the share purchase

The return is therefore calculated according to the increase of the stock price and the remunerated value of the investor.

(e) *Price multiples*—are calculated by relating the market price of the share to various elements that can be taken from the issuer's financial statements. Price multiples are easy to calculate and widely used indicators in making the investment decision.

The PER (price to earnings ratio) is the most widely used indicator to characterize the efficiency of investing.

$$PER = \frac{Cz}{Pn}$$

- PER—capitalization multiplier coefficient.
- Cz—the average price of the share within a trading day.
- Pn—net profit per share.

PER shows how much an investor must pay per share to get a monetary unit from the issuing company's profits. When the PER is relatively large, the stock is expensive, it can be overvalued, so owning it would no longer be justified; conversely, when the PER is relatively small, the stock is cheap, and it is recommended to buy it.

The coefficient is, in fact, the ratio between the issuer's market capitalization and the net profit and can be calculated using the issuer's net profit in the last 12 months or the estimated net profit for the next 12 months.

The use of PER has the advantages that it highlights the earning power of the company measured by the net profit related to an ordinary share issued. The indicator is highly appreciated among investors, and from a statistical point of view PER is strongly correlated with the evolution of the stock exchange price of the stock.

On the other hand, the indicator has the disadvantage that it is inapplicable in the case of companies with losses, and in the case of volatile, extraordinary gains, the PER distorts the value of the company.

- *The PB* (price per book value) indicator is calculated as the ratio between the share price and the value of equity (assets – liabilities).

$$PB = \frac{\text{Stock Price}}{\text{Book value}}$$

* Book value = value of equity = assets – debts.

The advantages of this indicator can be summarized as follows: used when PER cannot be calculated; book value is a more stable size compared to net profit per share; statistically, PB is correlated with the evolution of the stock market price.

The main disadvantages of using PB are that book value does not accurately reflect intangible assets, such as human capital, and technological change and inflation can distort its calculation.

It is generally considered that a sub-unit PB is a buy signal of that share.

- *The PS (price to sales) indicator* is a less volatile indicator than the PER coefficient and is strongly correlated with the evolution of the stock price.

$$PS = \frac{\text{Market Price}}{\text{Total turnover per share}}$$

Disadvantages can be mentioned: the increase in sales, which does not necessarily lead to an increase in operating profit, and the fact that PS does not reflect the cost structure of the company.

- *The PCF (price to cash-flow) indicator* is a more complex indicator than those mentioned above and is calculated as the ratio between the market price and cash flow per share.

$$PCF = \frac{\text{Market Price}}{\text{Cash flowper share}}$$

where:

- CF = net profit + depreciation + depreciation.

The PCF indicator has several advantages such as: it is more stable than the others multiple, more difficult to handle accounting and is a strong correlated with the evolution of the stock market.

In conclusion, all these indicators are highly relevant when comparing issuers within the same industry or at least within the same geographical region.

4.2.1 Solved Problems

1. What is the profit per share for a company with net profit of 235,800-euro profit, given that there are 120,000 shares on the market?
2. What is the dividend distribution rate for a company with net dividends (calculated after payment of dividend tax) of $45,000 which has a net profit of $234,980?
3. What is the dividend per share for a company with 1.3 mil. Shares if the net profit distributed to shareholders is $540,000?
4. A stock has brought, for 3 years, the annual dividends of 6 lei, 8 lei and 10 lei and is sold at 3 years from the date of purchase at the price of 120 lei. Determine the price for which the stock was bought, if the annual percentage rate was constant 6%.

$$PV = \frac{6}{1+0.06} + \frac{8}{(1+0.06)^2} + \frac{10}{(1+0.06)^3} + \frac{120}{(1+0.06)^3}$$

$$PV = \frac{6}{1.06} + \frac{8}{(1.06)^2} + \frac{130}{(1.06)^3} = 121.93$$

5. A stock has brought, for 20 years, constant annual dividends of 10 USD and it is sold after 20 years with 2000 USD. Determine the price for which the stock was bought, if the annual percentage rate was constant 6%.

$$PV = \frac{10}{1+0.06} + \frac{10}{(1+0.06)^2} + \ldots + \frac{10}{(1+0.06)^{20}} + \frac{2000}{(1+0.06)^{20}}$$

$$PV = 10\left(\frac{1}{1.06} + \frac{1}{(1.06)^2} + \ldots + \frac{1}{(1.06)^{20}}\right) + \frac{2000}{(1.06)^{20}}$$

$$PV = 10\left(\frac{1-\frac{1}{1.06^{21}}}{1-\frac{1}{1.06}} - 1\right) + \frac{2000}{(1.06)^{20}}$$

$$PV = 114.69 + 623.60$$

$$PV = 738.29 \text{ USD}$$

6. A stock was bought for 1760 lei and sold for 2240 lei after 8 years. Find the constant dividend, given that the interest rate during the whole period was constant 3.5%.

$$PV = \frac{D}{1+0.035} + \frac{D}{(1+0.035)^2} + \ldots + \frac{D}{(1+0.035)^8} + \frac{2240}{(1+0.035)^8}$$

$$1760 = D\left(\frac{1}{1.035} + \frac{1}{(1.035)^2} + \ldots + \frac{1}{(1.035)^8}\right) + \frac{2240}{(1.035)^8}$$

$$1760 = D \cdot \left(\frac{1-\frac{1}{1.035^9}}{1-\frac{1}{1.035}} - 1\right) + \frac{2240}{(1.035)^8}$$

$$1760 = D \cdot (6.87) + \frac{2240}{(1.035)^8}$$

$$D = \frac{1760 - \dfrac{2240}{(1.035)^8}}{6.87}$$

$$D = \frac{58.91}{6.87} = 8.57 \text{ lei}.$$

4.2.2 Applications

1. A stock has brought, for 5 years, the annual dividends of 16 lei, 18 lei, 14 lei, 15 lei and 10 lei and is sold 5 years from the date of purchase at the price of 1120 lei. Determine the price for which the stock was bought, if the annual percentage rate was constant 4.5%.
2. A stock has brought, for 12 years, constant annual dividends of 12 USD and is sold after 12 years with 1200 USD. Determine the price for which the stock was bought, if the annual percentage rate was constant 5.2%.
3. A stock was bought for 196 lei and sold for 224 lei after 7 years. Find the constant dividend, given that the interest rate during the whole period was constant 2.5%.
4. A stock has brought, for 6 years, constant annual dividends of 26 lei and is sold after 6 years at the price of 520 lei. Determine the price for which the stock was bought, if the annual percentage rate was constant 2.8%.
5. A stock has brought, for 15 years, constant annual dividends of 8 USD and is sold after 15 years with 1000 USD. Determine the price for which the stock was bought, if the annual percentage rate was constant 4.2%.
6. A stock was bought for 1926 euro and sold for 2024 euro after 11 years. Find the constant dividend, given that the interest rate during the whole period was constant 3.2%.
7. What is the present value of a stock with constant dividend of 24$ which is kept indefinite number of years at 3.5 annual percentage rate?

8. What is the present value of a stock with dividend 18 euros, which is constantly growing by 2%, which is kept indefinite number of years at 4%?

Useful Formulas for Problems 1–3

$$PPA = \frac{PN}{N}$$

- PPA—profit per share
- PN—net profit
- N—the total number of shares on the market

$$d = \frac{Dn}{Pn} \times 100$$

- d—the dividend distribution rate
- Dn—net dividends (calculated after the payment of the tax on dividends)
- Pn—net profit

$$DPA = \frac{Pnr}{N}$$

- DPA—dividend per share
- Pnr—the net profit distributed to the shareholders
- N—the total number of shares on the market

Useful Formula for Problems 4–6

$$PV = \frac{D_1}{1+k_1} + \frac{D_2}{(1+k_2)^2} + \ldots + \frac{D_n}{(1+k_n)^n} + \frac{FV}{(1+k_n)^n}$$

$$\sum_{t=1}^{n} a^t = a + (a)^2 + \ldots + (a)^n = a\left(1 + a + (a)^2 + \ldots + a^{n-1}\right) = a\frac{1-a^n}{1-a}$$

$$\sum_{t=1}^{n} a^t = a + (a)^2 + \ldots + (a)^n = 1 + a + (a)^2 + \ldots + (a)^n - 1$$

$$= \left(1 + a + (a)^2 + \ldots + a^{n-1} + a^n - 1\right) = \frac{1-a^{n+1}}{1-a} - 1$$

$$= \frac{1-a^{n+1}}{1-a} - 1 = \frac{1-a^{n+1} - 1 + a}{1-a} = \frac{a - a^{n+1}}{1-a} = a\frac{1-a^n}{1-a}$$

$$\sum_{t=1}^{n} \frac{1}{(1+k)^t} = \frac{1}{1+k} + \left(\frac{1}{1+k}\right)^2 + \ldots + \left(\frac{1}{1+k}\right)^n$$

$$= \frac{1}{k}\left(1 - \frac{1}{(1+k)^n}\right) = \left(\frac{1 - \frac{1}{(1+k)^{n+1}}}{1 - \frac{1}{1+k}} - 1\right)$$

4.3 Dividend Valuation Models

The expected dividends in the future are calculated by updating the cash flows, representing the future fructification of the investment through dividends.

$$V = \sum_{i=1}^{\infty} \frac{D_i}{(1+k)^i}$$

- *V*—the value of a share.
- D_i—Dividends at time *i*, understood as expected cash flows in the future.
- *k*—profitability required by shareholders; *i*—1, 2, …

Therefore, the value of a share can be calculated as the sum of the present values of the dividends expected in the future.

If the issuing company knows a regular development, it is assumed that dividends increase every year at an average rate g.

In this case, the present value of a share or its price (C) is equal to:

$$C = \frac{D_1}{(k-g)}$$

- D_1—dividends to be distributed in the following year ($t = 1$)
- k—the rate of return required by the shareholders
- g—increase of the dividend in year t compared to the previous year

The expected profitability of the shareholders is given by the relation:

$$k = g + \frac{D_1}{C}$$

- D_1/C expresses the dividend yield of the share.

The coefficient g can be interpreted at the same time as the expected performance in terms of annual stock market profit. This dividend growth rate is difficult to assess. It depends on the growth potential, expressed mainly by the evolution of turnover and results.

Assuming a regular dividend policy, the increase in dividends will be equal in the medium term to that of earnings per share. Such an assessment leads to results closer to reality than a simple assessment of trends in previous years. It is sometimes preferable to consider the rate of growth that has been achieved in recent years as the expected growth rate. Taking the example of a joint stock company that has overcome the phase of very strong growth, the g rate, which was previously very high, will decrease in the coming years. If the evaluation is done by extrapolating the trends, an exaggerated size of k is reached. Conversely, a joint stock company that has experienced difficulties and has had to reduce its share of the distributed profit has a negative dividend growth rate. Incorporating a negative value of *g* in the calculation of the required return leads to the conclusion that shareholders will lose.

To calculate the expected dividends in the future, several models are presented in the specialized literature, among which the ones described by William Sharpe and Gordon Alexander can be noticed.

4.3.1 Zero Growth Model

In this case, the dividends are constant from 1 year to the next.
$D0 = D1 = D2 = \ldots$
So, the dividend growth rate will be $gt = 0$ and we will have $D_t = D_{t-1}$
The value of a share will be:

$$V = \sum_{t=1}^{\infty} \frac{D_0}{(1+k)^t} = D_0 \left[\sum_{t=1}^{\infty} \frac{1}{(1+k)^t} \right]$$

Using the properties of infinite series of numbers, since $k > 0$, we obtain:

$$\sum_{t=1}^{\infty} \frac{1}{(1+k)^t} = \frac{1}{k}$$

Replacing in the original formula, it results:

$$V = \frac{D_0}{k}$$

In order to find out the profitability required by the shareholders (k^*), the value of the share with the stock price is replaced in the above relation.

$$P = \frac{D_0}{k^*} \Rightarrow k^* = \frac{D_0}{P}$$

- *P*—share price (stock price).

4.3.2 Constant Growth Model

The issuing company has a regular development, and it is assumed that dividends increase every year at an average rate g.

Thus, dividends will have the following evolution:

D_0—last year's dividend (last dividend paid) $D_1 = D_0(1 + g)$
$D_2 = D_1(1 + g) = D_0(1 + g)^2$
....
$D_t = D_{t-1}(1 + g) = D_0(1 + g)^t$ where:

D_t—dividend of year t.

The current value of an action is:

$$V = \sum_{t=1}^{\infty} \frac{D_0(1+g)^t}{(1+k)^t}$$

Where:

- k—profitability required by shareholders.

As D_0 is a constant, the value of the action becomes:

$$V = D_0 \left[\sum_{t=1}^{\infty} \frac{(1+g)^t}{(1+k)^t} \right]$$

Since $k > g$ and using the properties of infinite series of numbers in mathematics, equality is established:

$$\sum_{t=1}^{\infty} \frac{(1+g)^t}{(1+k)^t} = \frac{1+g}{k-g}$$

Replacing in the initial relationship, it results:

$$V = D_0\left(\frac{1+g}{k-g}\right), \text{relationship that can be written:}$$

$$V = \frac{D_1}{k-g}, \text{because}$$

$$D_1 = D_0(1+g)$$

The rate of return required by shareholders is:

$$P = D_0\left(\frac{1+g}{k^*-g}\right) \Rightarrow k^* = \frac{D_0(1+g)}{P} + g = \frac{D_1}{P} + g$$

$$\Rightarrow k^* = \frac{D_1}{P} + g$$

Where:

- k^*—profitability required by shareholders
- D_1—dividend of year 1
- P—stock exchange price of the action
- g—dividend growth rate

4.3.3 Multiple Growth Model

This model assumes finding a moment in the future after which dividends will increase at a constant average rate g. If we denote this future moment by T, then dividends D_1, D_2, D_T will be provided separately by the investor. Thereafter, dividends that are considered to increase at a constant rate g will be forecast as follows:

$$D_{T+1} = D_T(1+g)$$
$$D_{T+2} = D_{T+1}(1+g) = D_T(1+g)^2$$
$$D_{T+3} = D_{T+2}(1+g) = D_T(1+g)^3$$
....

To find out the present value of the share, the dividends are updated differently, dividing them into two groups:

- In the first situation, the dividends received up to and including T are updated.

This value is denoted by V_T.

$$V_T = \sum_{t=1}^{T} \frac{D_t}{(1+k)^t}$$

In the second situation, the dividends distributed after time T are updated. It is also considered that the investor is not at time $t = 0$, but at time $t = T$ (1). At this time ($t = T$) the dividends are updated according to the constant growth model, and this value obtained will be updated at time $t = 0$ (2).

$$V_T = D_{T+1}\left(\frac{1}{k-g}\right)$$

$$V_{T+1} = V_T \left[\frac{1}{(1+k)^T}\right] = \frac{D_{T+1}}{(k-g)(1+k)^T}$$

With the two values V_T and $V_T + 1$, the updated value of the action will be:

$$V = V_T + V_{T+1} = \sum_{t=1}^{T} \frac{D_t}{(1+k)^t} + \frac{D_{T+1}}{(k-g)(1+k)^T}$$

In order to determine the rate of return required by the shareholders, the relation is used:

$$P = \sum_{t=1}^{T} \frac{D_t}{\left(1+k^*\right)^t} + \frac{D_{T+1}}{\left(k^* - g\right)\left(1+k^*\right)^T}$$

Where:

- P—stock exchange price of the action
- k^*—the rate of return required by the shareholders

From this relationship, the rate of return required by shareholders cannot be deduced mathematically.

However, it can be expressed by the test method, by which its value can be approximated.

4.4 Valuation Based on a Finite Holding Period

So far, the situation in which an investor wants to invest indefinitely (long-term) has been analyzed. It will further analyze the situation in which an investor wants to invest in the short term, let us say for a period of 1 year.

The updated value of the action will be:

$$V = \frac{D_1 + P_1}{\left(1+k\right)} = \frac{D_1}{1+k} + \frac{P_1}{1+k}$$

Where:

- D_1—the forecasted dividend for the considered period
- P_1—forecast sales price
- k—profitability required by shareholders

In this situation, however, the price of P_1 is not known, which will be estimated based on the previous methods at time $t = 1$.

$$P_1 = \frac{D_2}{(1+k)^1} + \frac{D_3}{(1+k)^2} + \frac{D_4}{(1+k)^3} + \ldots = \sum_{t=2}^{\infty} \frac{D_t}{(1+k)^{t-1}}$$

Replace P_1 in the first relation:

$$V = \frac{D_1}{(1+k)} + \left[\frac{D_2}{(1+k)^1} + \frac{D_3}{(1+k)^2} + \frac{D_4}{(1+k)^3} + \ldots\right]\left(\frac{1}{1+k}\right)$$

$$= \frac{D_1}{(1+k)} + \frac{D_2}{(1+k)^1} + \frac{D_3}{(1+k)^2} + \frac{D_4}{(1+k)^3} + \ldots = \sum_{t=1}^{\infty} \frac{D_t}{(1+k)^t}$$

This relationship is identical to that obtained in the case of an unlimited investment. However, by valuing a share for a specified period in the future on the basis of future dividends and the estimated selling price, a value is obtained that is equal to that which would be obtained if the share were valued considering all future dividends.

The models for evaluating the actions for an unlimited term also allow *the determination of the PER coefficient.* These methods are based on the forecast of future net earnings per share. (E_t—net profit per share in year t).

Thus, the dividend of year t will be:

$$D_t = d_t \times E_t$$

Where:

- D_t—dividend of year t
- d_t—dividend distribution rate in year t
- E_t—net profit per share of year t

Substituting the value of the dividend into the equation of the present value of a share (P_1), we get:

$$P_1 = \frac{D_1}{(1+k)^1} + \frac{D_2}{(1+k)^2} + \frac{D_3}{(1+k)^3} + \ldots$$
$$= \frac{d_1 E_1}{(1+k)^1} + \frac{d_2 E_2}{(1+k)^2} + \frac{d_3 E_3}{(1+k)^3} + \ldots = \sum_{t=1}^{\infty} \frac{d_t E_t}{(1+k)^t}$$

We will note the growth rate of profit per share in year t compared to year t–1 with get. Thus $E_t = E_{t-1}(1 + g_{et})$

$E_1 = E_0(1 + g_{e1})$
$E_2 = E_1(1 + g_{e2}) = E_0(1 + g_{e1})(1 + g_{e2})$
$E_3 = E_2(1 + g_{e3}) = E_0(1 + g_{e1})(1 + g_{e2})(1 + g_{e3})$
....

Substituting in relation (3), we obtain:

$$V = \frac{d_1 \left[E_0 (1+g_{e1}) \right]}{(1+k)^1} + \frac{d_2 \left[E_0 (1+g_{e1})(1+g_{e2}) \right]}{(1+k)^2} + \ldots$$

In the above relation, E_0 comes out as a common factor and results in:

$$\frac{V}{E_0} = \frac{d_1 (1+g_{e1})}{(1+k)^1} + \frac{d_2 (1+g_{e1})(1+g_{e2})}{(1+k)^2} + \ldots$$

But $\dfrac{V}{E_0} = \text{PER} \Rightarrow$

$$\text{PER} = \frac{d_1 (1+g_{e1})}{(1+k)^1} + \frac{d_2 (1+g_{e1})(1+g_{e2})}{(1+k)^2} + \ldots$$

According to the above relationship, PER will increase if:

- Increases the dividend distribution rate
- Increases the growth rate of net profit per share
- Decreases the profitability required by shareholders

In practice, however, if a company wants to increase the share price by increasing the dividend distribution rate ($d_1, d_2, d_3, \ldots$), this will lead to a decrease in the growth rate of net profit per share ($g_{e1}, g_{e2}, g_{e3}, \ldots$) and, considering that the company maintains the same investment policy, this will have the effect of remaining unchanged in the share price.

In the Zero-Growth Model it is considered that the net profit per share remains constant from 1 year to another, so $d_t = 1$ and $E_0 = E_1 = E_2 = \ldots$ It is also considered that the company distributes all net profit per share in the form of dividends, $E_0 = D_1 = E_1 = D_2 = E_2 = \ldots$ This assumption is made because, if the company reinvested part of the profit, it would lead to the increase of future profits, so the hypothesis would no longer be true.

$$V = \sum_{t=1}^{\infty} \frac{D_0}{(1+k)^t} = D_0 \left[\sum_{t=1}^{\infty} \frac{1}{(1+k)^t} \right] = \frac{D_0}{k} = \frac{E_0}{k} \Rightarrow V = \frac{E_0}{k}$$

So,

$$\text{PER} = \frac{V}{E_0} = \frac{1}{k}$$

where:

* V—the current value of the action
* E_0—net profit per share
* k—profitability required by shareholders

In The Constant-Growth Model, the rate of increase in net profit per share is noted and the dividend distribution rate (d) is considered to be constant.

So: $E_1 = E_0(1 + g_e)$
$E_2 = E_1(1 + g_e) = E_0(1 + g_e)^2$
$E_3 = E_2(1 + g_e) = E_0(1 + g_e)^3$
....
$E_t = E_0(1 + g_e)^t$

But:

$$V = \sum_{t=1}^{\infty} \frac{d \times E_t}{(1+k)^t} \Rightarrow V = \sum_{t=1}^{\infty} \frac{d \times E_0 (1+g_e)^t}{(1+k)^t}$$

Because $d \times E_0$ = constant, then:

$$V = d \times E_0 \left[\sum_{t=1}^{\infty} \frac{(1+g_e)^t}{(1+k)^t} \right]$$

According to the properties of infinite series of numbers, it results:

$$\sum_{t=1}^{\infty} \frac{(1+g_e)^t}{(1+k)^t} = \frac{1+g_e}{k-g_e} \Rightarrow V = d \times E_0 \left(\frac{1+g_e}{k-g_e} \right)$$

4.4.1 Solved Problems

1. A stock has brought, for 30 years, constant annual dividends of 10 USD and is sold after 30 years with 2000 USD. Determine the price for which the stock was bought, if the annual percentage rate was constant 4%.

$$V = \frac{D}{k} \left(1 - \frac{1}{(1+k)^n} \right) + \frac{FV}{(1+k)^n} = D \left(\frac{1 - \frac{1}{(1+k)^{n+1}}}{1 - \frac{1}{1+k}} - 1 \right) + \frac{FV}{(1+k)^n}$$

$$V = \frac{10}{0.04} \cdot \left(1 - \frac{1}{(1.04)^{30}} \right) + \frac{2{,}000}{(1.04)^{30}}$$

$$V = 789.56$$

2. What is the present value of a stock for which the rate of return required by the shareholders is 5% in the following cases.

(a) The dividend is constantly 20 lei.
(b) The dividend in the previous year was 10 lei and it increases at a constant rate of 4%.
(c) The dividend in the previous year was 8 lei, for 5 years the dividend is constant, after which it increases with a constant rate of 2%.

a) $V = \sum_{t=1}^{\infty} \frac{D}{(1+k)^t} = \lim_{n \to \infty} \frac{D}{k} \cdot \left(1 - \frac{1}{(1+k)^n}\right) = \frac{D}{k}$

$$V = \frac{20}{0.05} = 400 \text{ lei}$$

b) $V = \sum_{t=1}^{\infty} \frac{D_0}{(1+k)^t} = D_0 \cdot \lim_{n \to \infty} \frac{1+g}{k-g} \cdot \left[1 - \left(\frac{1+g}{1+k}\right)^n\right], g < k$

$$= 10 \cdot \frac{1 + 0.04}{0.05 - 0.04}$$

$$= 10 \cdot \frac{1.04}{0.01} = 1{,}040 \text{ lei}$$

c) $V = \frac{D}{k} \cdot \left[\left(1 - \frac{1}{(1+k)^T}\right) + \frac{1+g}{(1+k)^T} \cdot \frac{1}{(k-g)}\right]$

$$V = \frac{8}{0.05} \cdot \left[\left(1 - \frac{1}{(1.05)^5}\right) + \frac{1.02}{(1.05)^5} \cdot \frac{1}{(0.05 - 0.02)}\right]$$

$$V = 4297.02$$

4.4.2 Applications

1. What is the present value of a stock for which the rate of return required by the shareholders is 6% in the following cases.

   (a) The dividend is constant 12 euro.
   (b) The dividend in the previous year was 10 euro and it increases at a constant rate of 3%.
   (c) The dividend in the previous year was 8 euro, for 8 years the dividend is constant, after that a perpetuity with constant growth 4%.

2. What is the present value of a stock for which the rate of return required by the shareholders is 9% in the following cases.

   (a) The dividend is constantly 10 USD.
   (b) The dividend in the previous year was 8 USD and it increases at a constant rate of 4%.
   (c) The dividend in the previous year was 9 USD, for 10 years the dividend is constant, after that a perpetuity with constant growth 3%.

3. What is the present value of a stock for which the rate of return required by the shareholders is 12% in the following cases.

   (a) The dividend is constantly 20 lei.
   (b) The dividend in the previous year was 16 lei and it increases at a constant rate of 5%.
   (c) The dividend in the previous year was 12 lei, for 6 years the dividend is constant, after that a perpetuity with constant growth of 5%.

4. What is the present value of a stock for which the rate of return required by the shareholders is 7% in the following cases.

   (a) The dividend is constant 20 lei in the first 4 years, then it increases by 2% in the next 6 years and after that a perpetuity with constant growth of 3%.

(b) The dividend is constant 10 lei in the first 3 years, then it is constant at 15 lei for the next 4 years and after that a perpetuity with constant growth of 4%.

a) $V = \dfrac{D}{1+k} + \dfrac{D}{(1+k)^2} + \ldots + \dfrac{D}{(1+k)^4}$

$\underbrace{}_{4\ years}$

$+ \dfrac{D(1+g_1)}{(1+k)^{4+1}} + \dfrac{D(1+g_1)^2}{(1+k)^{4+2}} + \ldots + \dfrac{D(1+g_1)^6}{(1+k)^{4+6}} +$

$\underbrace{}_{next\ 6\ years}$

$+ \dfrac{D(1+g_1)^6(1+g_2)}{(1+k)^{10+1}} + \dfrac{D(1+g_1)^6(1+g_2)^2}{(1+k)^{10+2}} + \ldots$

$\underbrace{}_{next\ n-10\ year}$

$V = D\left(\dfrac{1}{1+k} + \left(\dfrac{1}{1+k}\right)^2 + \left(\dfrac{1}{1+k}\right)^3 + \left(\dfrac{1}{1+k}\right)^4\right)$

$+ D\left(\left(\dfrac{1}{1+k}\right)^5 (1+g_1) + \ldots + \left(\dfrac{1}{1+k}\right)^{10} (1+g_1)^6\right)$

$+ D\left(\left(\dfrac{1}{1+k}\right)^{11} (1+g_2)^7 + \ldots + \left(\dfrac{1}{1+k}\right)^{n-10} (1+g_2)^{n-10}\right)$

$V = D\left(\dfrac{1}{1+k} + \left(\dfrac{1}{1+k}\right)^2 + \left(\dfrac{1}{1+k}\right)^3 + \left(\dfrac{1}{1+k}\right)^4\right)$

$+ D\dfrac{1}{(1+k)^4}\left(\left(\dfrac{1+g_1}{1+k}\right)^1 + \ldots + \left(\dfrac{1+g_1}{1+k}\right)^6\right)$

$+ D\dfrac{(1+g_1)^6}{(1+k)^{10}} \lim_{n\to\infty}\left(\left(\dfrac{1+g_2}{1+k}\right)^1 + \ldots + \left(\dfrac{1+g_2}{1+k}\right)^{n-10}\right)$

$$V = D\left(\frac{1}{1+k} + \left(\frac{1}{1+k}\right)^2 + \left(\frac{1}{1+k}\right)^3 + \left(\frac{1}{1+k}\right)^4\right)$$

$$+ D\frac{1}{(1+k)^4}\left(\left(\frac{1+g_1}{1+k}\right)^1 + \ldots + \left(\frac{1+g_1}{1+k}\right)^6\right)$$

$$+ D \cdot \frac{(1+g_1)^6(1+g_2)}{(1+k)^{10}} \cdot \frac{1}{(k-g)}$$

$$V = \frac{D}{k}\cdot\left(1 - \frac{1}{(1+k)^4}\right) + D\frac{1}{(1+k)^4} \cdot \frac{1+g_1}{k-g_1}\cdot\left[1 - \left(\frac{1+g_1}{1+k}\right)^6\right]$$

$$+ D \cdot \frac{(1+g_1)^6(1+g_2)}{(1+k)^{10}} \cdot \frac{1}{(k-g_2)}$$

$$V = \frac{20}{0.07}\cdot\left(1 - \frac{1}{(1.07)^4}\right) + 20\frac{1}{(1.07)^4} \cdot \frac{1.02}{0.07-0.02}\cdot\left[1 - \left(\frac{1.02}{1.07}\right)^6\right]$$

$$+ 20 \cdot \frac{(1.02)^6(1.03)}{(1.07)^{10}} \cdot \frac{1}{(0.07-.03)}$$

b) $V = D_1 \cdot \left(\frac{1}{1+k} + \left(\frac{1}{1+k}\right)^2 + \left(\frac{1}{1+k}\right)^3\right)$

$$+ D_2 \cdot \left(\left(\frac{1}{1+k}\right)^4 + \ldots + \left(\frac{1}{1+k}\right)^7\right) + D_2 \cdot \left[\frac{1+g}{(1+k)^8} \cdot \frac{1}{(k-g)}\right]$$

5. What is the present value of a stock for which the rate of return required by the shareholders is 8% in the following cases.

   (a) The dividend is constant 16 euros in the first 5 years, then it increases by 3% in the next 4 years and after that a perpetuity with constant growth of 4%.
   (b) The dividend is constant 22 euros in the first 8 years, then it is constant at 25 euros for the next 5 years and after that a perpetuity with constant growth of 2%.

5

Bond Market

As seen in the previous chapter, shares are a form of permanent capital that is returned only in special situations, and the premise is that it will never be repaid. Bonds, on the other hand, are a form of loan. They are funds borrowed by an organization at a certain interest that is paid periodically, having a fixed repayment date.

Although, in essence, they are "loan funds," the bonds have as specific elements:

- Long maturity—normally between 5 and 20 years.
- Negotiable character, being able to be sold/bought on the secondary market.

The duration for which the bonds are issued is an important aspect, without considering their ability to be traded, the bonds can be seen as a long-term loan between two parties. This would mean that the terms of the loan will be set by the lender, who will have some degree of control over the debtor's business.

The result is that the funds obtained by issuing bonds can be used for any purpose, and their early repayment can be requested by the creditor only in exceptional cases. Therefore, these funds are considered "permanent" over the life of the bonds. Often, the repayment of funds is done through a new bond issue, the real term for which funds are attracted being "indefinite" for the issuer.

The bond issue is preferred to the share issue for the following reasons:

1. Some organizations, such as government and local government authorities, cannot issue shares on their own account and must issue bonds to secure funding.
2. Bond issues are generally cheaper than equity issues.
3. The annual cost of a bond is fixed and should be less than the benefits obtained by using the funds, thus increasing the profit obtained by the shareholders of the company who benefited from financing through the issuance of bonds. This effect is known as the degree of gearing.
4. The interest paid for the bond is deducted from the profit before its taxation, while the dividend paid for the share involves the distribution of net profits (after tax).
5. The mechanism for issuing bonds is similar to that specific to issuing shares. A significant difference between the two mechanisms is the content of the contract that must accompany the issuance of bonds. Thus, the issuance contract includes specifications regarding:

    * The rights and obligations of the issuing company and of the bondholders.
    * Details related to the characteristics of the bonds—the terms of payment of interest, the manner of establishing the provisions for the situations in which the issuer does not honor its payment obligations at maturity, special clauses regarding the repayment of the loan, etc..
    * Issue structure.
    * The identity and responsibilities of those who supervise compliance with the issuance contract.
    * How to guarantee the title, if applicable.

5.1 Bond Structure

All bonds are based on a common structure, namely: the bond includes a capital component and an interest component. As in the case of a treasury bill or bill of exchange, the capital component of the bond consists of a loan for a predetermined period, a loan granted to the issuer by the investor.

The bondholder receives an interest periodically, set as a rate at face value. This income obtained by the investor is called a coupon, a name that derives from the fact that the payment was traditionally made against a coupon attached in the form of an extension to the bond itself.

(a) *The face value* (par value, face value or nominal value) is the amount of money that the bond issuer (debtor) will pay at maturity. The nominal value or the par value is determined as follows:

$$NV = \frac{LV}{N}$$

where:

- *NV*—face value
- *LV*—loan amount
- *N*—number of bonds issued

(b) *The coupon* is the generic name for the payment of interest related to financial investments in bonds. It represents the periodic income that the bondholder receives, and is determined as a percentage (coupon rate) applied to the nominal value, illustrated in the relation below:

$$C = c \times NV$$

where:

- *C*—coupon
- *c*—coupon rate
- *NV*—nominal value

For most bonds, interest payments are made annually, although semi-annual payments (every 6 months) have begun to become more common. They are much less common, monthly or 3-month interest payments.

(c) *Maturity* is another characteristic element of the bonds that represent the period of time for which the loan is granted and in which the interest coupons are paid. The bonds are issued on certain maturities depending on the capital requirement of the issuer. For example, the state may issue treasury bills on maturities of less than 1 year, treasury bills between 1 year and 10 years (medium term), and long-term bonds between 10 and 30 years.

The bond has a market value that is usually different from the face value. The market value of the bond varies depending on changes in market interest rates. The main reason why the market value may differ from the nominal value is determined by the interest rate. The interest rate set for bonds is fixed, so the absolute interest received by the investor does not vary. The change in market interest rates influences the expectations of potential investors in bonds regarding the volume of profit they would potentially obtain by buying bonds. In order to obtain a certain expected profit, the price to be paid for the bond (market price) changes. Starting from the previous example, we assume that a potential investor wants to obtain a 15% return. For this, the annual interest received must represent 15% of the investment made, i.e., the price paid. In this case, the interest collected, calculated on an annual basis is:

$$1{,}000{,}000 \cdot 0.12 = 120{,}000 \text{ m.u.}$$

To determine the volume of capital corresponding to obtaining a yield of 15%, we divide the interest by the required yield:

$$\text{Market value} = \frac{120.000}{0.15} = 800.000 \text{ m.u.}$$

It is observed that the market value has decreased to allow the increase of the yield.

Thus, the market value of bonds will decrease when market interest rates rise and increase when rates fall (a process also found in the case of money market-specific instruments). Therefore, bondholders are exposed to risk as follows:

* The rate of return for the initial investment does not depend on changes in interest rates.
* The change in market value results in either a loss or a profit when the security is sold.

Both factors are very important, as they increase the attractiveness of bonds when market interest rates fall and interest rates fall when rates rise.

5.2 Types of Bonds

The obligations in the standard group are based on the issuance and trading of the techniques used since the beginning of the emergence of this long-term financing method. Their distinctive feature is that the mobilization of funds and the payment at maturity of investors is done directly and at pre-established values on the issue.

Although in financial practice they have different names, these bonds are known as standard (classical) bonds, all with the following standardized characteristics:

* The value of the coupon is fixed.
* The coupon is paid annually.
* The maturity is fixed.
* The amount paid on issue (principal) by the investor is the nominal value.
* The value at which the maturity obligation will be repurchased by the issuer is fixed.

- The characteristics of the bond cannot be changed during existence until maturity.
- The bond does not include, in addition to the rights resulting from the financing relationship, other additional rights for the investor.

In order to meet specific requirements of issuers and/or investors, over time, bonds have been created with characteristics different from the classic ones, in terms of:

- Coupon
- Maturity
- Issue price
- The redemption price
- Additional rights

Some types of bonds may have only one different characteristic from the standard ones, others have two different characteristics compared to the standard ones (for example, the zero-coupon bond that is issued at a substantial discount), or (less frequently) several features that differ from the standard ones.

Bonds often have different characteristics determined by the nationality of the issuer, the country where the issue takes place and the currency of the issue, which will be presented later in the session.

Variable coupon bonds are those in which the payment of interest—as a distribution over time, as well as the level of amounts paid may vary over the life of the bond—until maturity. Thus, the interest rate may vary until maturity, depending on the issuer's objectives. The most frequently issued are bonds with a variable coupon rate, respectively those in which, for a first period of time, no coupon payments are made or those in which the amount paid and related to the coupon can increase or decrease throughout the period until maturity. These variations consider the characteristics of the cash flows generated by the investment made through the respective bond issue.

A variant of the variable coupon bond is *the floating rate coupon bonds*. This type of bond known as FMR (floating rate notes) is characterized by the fact that there is an automatic adjustment, at specified intervals, of the coupon interest rate according to the evolution of a reference interest rate, for example, LIBOR. In some cases, the fluctuation may be limited by stipulating in the issuance agreement a maximum ceiling (head), a minimum level (floor) or both (collar).

We can also encounter *indexed coupon rate bonds*, called indexed bonds. The income from these bonds varies depending on a particular indicator, for example, the retail price index or the stock market index. The purpose of such a bond is to provide investors with protection against inflation. In some countries, index-linked bonds are prohibited by law because they are considered to encourage inflation.

Another type of bond that deviates from the standard feature of the coupon is the *zero-coupon bond*. Zero-coupon bonds are those that do not involve interest payments during the period of existence and are issued with a significant discount. They are created on the basis of classical bonds, by dividing their value into a number of zero-coupon bonds, the number of the division being equal to the number of cash flows that the classic bond would generate. For example, from a classic 10-year bond with an annual payable coupon, 11 zero-coupon bonds can be created (10 corresponding to interest payments and one bond corresponding to the value of the investment). The process of creating zero-coupon bonds from classic bonds can be reversible.

For investors who are reluctant to risk, the zero-coupon bond is an alternative that eliminates the risk of reinvesting interest income. As for the issuers, they will proceed to "divide" a classic bond into bonds with zero coupon if the price you could get from selling zero-coupon bonds is higher than the base bond.

A more sophisticated form of *bond* is one that involves two currencies in which it is denominated: one currency is used to denominate the face value of the bond and another for the value of the coupon (dual currency bond). In this case, the payment of interest is made at an exchange rate that can be set at the date of issue, or the spot rate can be used from the date of payment. It is also possible for the currency in which the interest is paid to be changed in the period between issue and maturity, depending on the investor's option.

The bond with annuities is less used and is characterized by the fact that within the coupon payments is necessary a part of the amount initially invested, so that the repayment of the investment is made throughout the life of the bond, similar to repaying a loan. This type of bond is usually associated with issues intended to be used to finance projects that soon bring income (in the form of cash) that allows the repayment of loans along the way.

A less common type of bond is the profit-sharing obligation, which means that, if the issuer records certain predetermined financial results, compared to the fixed interest granted to the investor, he will receive an additional percentage of achievements. In some cases, the coupon may be reinvested in other bonds of the issuer, at the investor's choice. This process involves increasing the number of bonds held by the investor.

Another category of bonds are option bonds, which are known as LOBO and BOLO. LOBO (Lender's Option, Borrower's Option) allows the coupon rate to be set periodically at the investor's option, and the issuer has the option to accept this rate or repurchase the bond before maturity. The opposite variant is the BOLO (Borrower's Option, Lender's Option), in which the issuer periodically sets the coupon rate, and the investor has the possibility to either accept those rates or to ask the issuer to repurchase the bond before maturity.

For all types of bonds presented above, the coupon can be paid either in gross amount or in net amount, depending on the applicable legislation.

5.2.1 International Bonds

Bonds issued on the national market by national issuers and denominated in the national currency are domestic bonds. Those issued on a foreign market and denominated in the currency of the respective country are called foreign bonds. Bonds issued in an external market but denominated in a currency different from that of both the issuer's country and that of the investment market, make up the category of Eurobonds. For example, if an Italian company issues dollar-denominated bonds on the US market, we are talking about foreign bonds, but if the place of issue is Singapore, they are considered Eurobonds.

In order to distinguish between domestic bonds and bonds issued by foreign entities on the territory of a country and expressed in the national currency of that country, foreign bonds have specific names. We present, for example, the name under which foreign bonds are located on three main financial markets:

Country	Foreign Bonds
SUA	Yankee
Japan	Samurai
Great Britain	Bulldog

While these countries host the main financial centers on which Eurobonds are issued (London holding supremacy), the Eurobond market is in fact an electronic market, operating 24 h a day, with participants from all over the world communicating and trading by phone and computer.

The Eurobond market began to develop in the first years of the seventh decade. Until then, companies wishing to issue bonds denominated in currencies other than the national currency, in order to finance the development of activity abroad, had to resort to bond issuance. Bonds, which have three disadvantages:

- The cost related to the issuance process abroad is high.
- The legal framework and the fiscal regime in the country on whose market the launch of the issue is desired may be unattractive or may involve very high costs.
- The company may be unknown in that market.

While the Eurobond market has experienced significant development, the foreign bond market has been on a downward trend. Foreign bonds are still used to attract foreign currency capital, but have two disadvantages compared to Eurobonds:

(a) Euro bonds are usually issued simultaneously in several countries, while foreign bonds—themselves—can only be issued in one country. This greatly influences the liquidity of securities.

(b) Eurobonds are not subject to the regulations of the country in which the issue takes place, including the income tax from the investment in Eurobonds. Foreign bonds are under the tax jurisdiction of the country in which they are issued.

In this context, it is noted that some large companies, such as Volvo, can issue foreign bonds in the countries in which they intend to invest, but most of its international bond issues are Eurobonds. It is interesting to note that European companies, such as Volvo, represent a small segment of the Eurobond market. The largest share in this market is held by American and Japanese companies, followed by banks, governments, and international financial bodies, such as the World Bank and the European Investment Bank.

In part, the presence of American companies in this market is motivated by their preference for financing through bond loans, compared to bank loans. In the USA, about 70% of the funds attracted by companies are sourced by bonds, the difference being bank loans. In Europe, the proportion is reversed, which explains the low share of companies' financing through Eurobonds.

Under such circumstances, it may seem somewhat unnatural for London to be the main center for Eurobonds. However, approximately 20% of the ISMA (International Secondary Markets Association) member companies and 70% of the dealers/marketers belonging to this association are headquartered in London. One of the reasons may be that London is the place where the introduction and, later, development of Eurobonds and Eurobond markets was initiated. On the other hand, the London market has the strongest international character among the main world financial markets.

5.3 Clauses Associated with the Bonds

To be more attractive to investors, bonds sometimes have certain clauses associated with them. These clauses are exercised only if certain events occur, therefore we can say that bonds with clauses behave like option contracts.

- Redemption clause at the initiative of the issuer (Callable bonds). If a company issues bonds at a certain coupon rate, and market interest rates fall, then bond financing becomes expensive. Thus, the company can repurchase bonds and issue new bonds at a lower coupon rate (more advantageous financing). To be attractive to investors, there is a certain fixed period in which the company cannot redeem its bonds.
- Redemption clause at the initiative of the bondholder (Puttable bonds). Bondholders may decide whether to redeem them until maturity, maturity or later. For example, if a bond with a redemption clause offers coupons higher than other returns on various investments, it will choose to extend the maturity of the bond.
- The convertibility clause by which the bondholder can convert the bonds he holds into shares at a certain conversion rate. Any investor will exercise the associated clause only if the market value of the shares of the issuing company is higher than the market value of the bonds held. Most bonds that have associated with the convertibility clause offer very small coupons and lower yields at maturity than non-convertible bonds (which is why they are also said to be deep out of the money). Therefore, the conversion rate is set so that the investor does not immediately exercise the convertibility clause.

Example: Suppose an investor holds a bond (VN = 1000 EUR) that has the convertibility clause associated with it, and the conversion rate is 1 bond for every 10 shares. The price of the bond is currently 873 EUR. The exercise of the convertibility clause is performed by the investor if the share price is higher than

$$\frac{\text{Bond price} \cdot \text{number of bonds}}{\text{conversion rate}} = \frac{873 \cdot 1}{10} = 87.3 \text{ euro}$$

i.e., shares are worth more than the bond. We notice that convertible bonds behave like option contracts.

- If the market price of the share is 65 EUR, then it is not appropriate to exercise the clause as these shares are worth and the bond

65 EUR × 10 shares = 650 EUR, has a higher market value of 873 EUR, respectively.
- If the share price is 122 EUR, then the market value of the shares is 1220 EUR and it is therefore appropriate to exercise the convertibility clause, the investor's profit being 347 EUR.

5.4 Additional Rights

Bonds may be accompanied by a document called a warrant which confers a certain right on their holder. Often, they can be traded separately from the basic title, with a secondary market for them.

The right offered by the warrant can be exercised at any time after a certain time (in which case the warrant is of American type) or only at certain specified dates (European type warrant).

Most warranties give the right to purchase equity warrants or debt warrants at certain predetermined prices. Less common are warrants that give the right to buy other forms of options or even goods.

These bonds are known as warrant bonds.

In general, the price at which shares may be purchased against the guarantor attached to a bond is that at the time the bond is issued. Thus, the right conferred by the warrant is expected to be exercised when the market value of the share's increases. This element adds attractiveness to the issuance of warrant bonds that entitle to the purchase of shares.

Regarding the warranties that give the right to purchase bonds, the most common types are:

- Warranties that give the right to purchase bonds identical to the support ones, at a specified price.
- Warranties that give the right to purchase bonds other than the support ones, at a specified price.
- Warranties that give the right to purchase other bonds if the underlying bonds are repurchased before maturity at the initiative of the issuer.

We have previously mentioned that warrants can often be detached from the underlying security and traded separately. In some cases, there is an option to sell them to the issuer at a predetermined price.

5.5 Factors that Influence and Determine the Value of Bonds

As we know, the required return is another way of looking at the interest rate that investors expect to receive as compensation for the investment made. Therefore, the factors that affect the return are among those that influence the interest rate required for any investment:

- Modification of the issuer's credit risk
- The forecasted evolution of the inflation rate
- The forecasted evolution of the market interest rate
- The remaining period until the maturity of the bonds
- Financial structure (implications determined by taxation)
- Market liquidity
- The forecasted evolution of exchange rates (if relevant)

(a) *The Issuer's Credit Risk*

One of the key factors related to the required return is the investor's perception of the issuer's credit risk. Like any creditor, investors demand a higher return to compensate them for taking a higher risk. This difference represents the risk premium and is directly related to the issuer's credit risk.

We can identify three categories of bonds that have distinct characteristics in terms of risk premium:

1. Government obligations are considered non-risky because they are guaranteed by the government. As a result, the yield they provide is the benchmark for the country's market.

2. Bonds issued by companies and secured by certain assets of that company present a low risk, which is reflected in a risk premium of several percentage points compared to the reference level. The credit risk of the major bond issuers is assessed by the rating agencies.
3. Unsecured bonds issued by companies are the riskiest and, in order to compensate for this element and to make it attractive to investors, the risk premium is high. In the literature, these bonds are found under the name of junk bonds. The risk premium for this type of bond starts at 5% from the reference level.

(b) *Inflation Rate*

The inflation rate affects the required return, because the income obtained by the investor must compensate the decrease of the relative value of the investment. One way to compensate for inflationary erosion is to add the forecast inflation rate to the required rate of return, thus obtaining a rate of return adjusted for the rate of inflation.

(c) *The Official Discount Rate*

The official discount rate or interest rate (Central Bank), which is the reference element in setting interest rates on the money and capital markets, also influences the level of return on bond investments.

(d) *The Remaining Period Until the Maturity of the Bonds*

As a bond approaches maturity, its market value tends to approach the redemption value. This phenomenon can be seen as the result of the action of two forces. On the one hand, when the maturity period falls below 1 year, the current (market) difference from the par value is reduced to ensure the required return calculated on an annualized (annualized) basis. On the other hand, at the time of redemption, the market value must be equal to the redemption value.

(e) Taxation-Induced Implications

Taxation of income from holding bonds can have a direct effect on the net income collected by the investor. An important element is the way the coupon is set: at net or gross value. Also, depending on the level of taxation of the investor, the actual income obtained can be substantially affected.

(f) Market Liquidity

If the relative liquidity decreases, the demand for funds increases, and the interest rate offered for attracting funds increases, so that the market value of the securities decreases.

(g) Exchange Rate

In situations where the bonds are denominated in foreign currency, the investor is exposed to currency risk. However, if the market perceives an appreciation of a currency against the national currency, the demand for bonds denominated in that currency will increase. This phenomenon leads to a reduction in the relative liquidity of bonds denominated in the national currency.

5.6 Financial Evaluation of the Bonds

$$P = \sum_{t=1}^{n} \frac{C_t}{(1+d)^t} = \frac{C_1}{(1+d)} + \frac{C_2}{(1+d)^2} + \ldots + \frac{C_n + VN}{(1+d)^n}$$

- P = price of the bond
- C_t = value of the coupon in year t
- VN = nominal value of the coupon or face value
- N = number of years
- d = interest rate

$$P = \frac{C}{(1+d)} + \frac{C}{(1+d)^2} + \ldots + \frac{C+VN}{(1+d)^n}$$

$$P = \frac{C}{(1+d)} + \frac{C}{(1+d)^2} + \ldots + \frac{C}{(1+d)^n} + \frac{VN}{(1+d)^n}$$

$$P = \frac{C}{(1+d)}\left[1 + \frac{1}{(1+d)} + \ldots + \frac{1}{(1+d)^{n-1}}\right] + \frac{VN}{(1+d)^n}$$

$$P = \frac{C}{(1+d)}\left[\frac{1-\dfrac{1}{(1+d)^n}}{1-\dfrac{1}{1+d}}\right] + \frac{VN}{(1+d)^n}$$

$$P = \frac{C}{(1+d)}\left[\frac{1-\dfrac{1}{(1+d)^n}}{\dfrac{1+d-1}{1+d}}\right] + \frac{VN}{(1+d)^n}$$

$$P = \frac{C}{(1+d)}\left[\frac{1-\dfrac{1}{(1+d)^n}}{\dfrac{d}{1+d}}\right] + \frac{VN}{(1+d)^n}$$

$$P = \frac{C}{(1+d)} \cdot \frac{1+d}{d} \cdot \left(1 - \frac{1}{(1+d)^n}\right) + \frac{VN}{(1+d)^n}$$

$$P = \frac{C}{d} \cdot \left(1 - \frac{1}{(1+d)^n}\right) + \frac{VN}{(1+d)^n}$$

Observation

If the interest rate is not constant in time, we have:

$$P = \sum_{t=1}^{n} \frac{C_t}{(1+d_t)^t} = \frac{C}{(1+d_1)} + \frac{C}{(1+d_1)(1+d_2)} + \ldots$$
$$+ \frac{C+VN}{(1+d_1)(1+d_2)\ldots(1+d_n)}$$

5.6.1 Solved Problems

1. Suppose an investor holds a classic bond with the following characteristics: face value 1000 USD, coupon rate 10%, coupon is paid annually, maturity 10 years, and interest rate: a) 5%; b) 8% and c) 10%. What is the price of the bond?

$$P = \frac{C}{d} \cdot \left(1 - \frac{1}{(1+d)^n}\right) + \frac{VN}{(1+d)^n}$$

$$P = \frac{100}{0.05} \cdot \left(1 - \frac{1}{(1.05)^{10}}\right) + \frac{1000}{(1.05)^{10}}$$

$$P = 1.386{,}09 \text{ USD}$$

2. Consider a classic bond with the nominal value 1200 EUR, coupon rate a) 6% and b) 9%, interest rate 6%, and maturity 8, 5 and 1 years. Determine its price.

$$P = \frac{C}{d} \cdot \left(1 - \frac{1}{(1+d)^n}\right) + \frac{VN}{(1+d)^n}$$

$$P = \frac{72}{0.06} \cdot \left(1 - \frac{1}{(1.06)^8}\right) + \frac{1200}{(1.06)^8}$$

$$P = 1200 \text{ EUR}$$

3. Company A issued a bond with the following characteristics: face value 1000 EUR, coupon rate 5%, (coupon is paid annually), maturity 8 years, interest 4%, repayment being made at maturity.

   Company B issues a bond with a coupon rate of 6%, a maturity of 8 years, the nominal value 800 EUR and the interest rate of 5%.

   What will investors prefer?

$$P_A = \frac{C}{d} \cdot \left(1 - \frac{1}{(1+d)^n}\right) + \frac{VN}{(1+d)^n}; C = \frac{c}{100} \cdot VN.$$

$$P_A = \frac{50}{0.04} \cdot \left(1 - \frac{1}{(1.04)^8}\right) + \frac{1000}{(1.04)^8}; C = \frac{5}{100} \cdot 1000 = 50$$

$$P_A = 1067.33 \text{ EUR}$$

$$P_B = \frac{C}{d} \cdot \left(1 - \frac{1}{(1+d)^n}\right) + \frac{VN}{(1+d)^n}; C = \frac{c}{100} \cdot VN.$$

$$P_B = \frac{48}{0.05} \cdot \left(1 - \frac{1}{(1.05)^8}\right) + \frac{800}{(1.05)^8}; C = \frac{6}{100} \cdot 800 = 48$$

$$P_B = 851.71 \text{ EUR}$$

4. What is the price of a zero-coupon bond with face value of $1000, evaluated for 6 years with interest rate of 2%?

$$P = \frac{0}{(1+d)} + \frac{0}{(1+d)^2} + \ldots + \frac{0+VN}{(1+d)^n}$$

$$P = \frac{0}{d} \cdot \left(1 - \frac{1}{(1+d)^n}\right) + \frac{VN}{(1+d)^n}$$

$$P = \frac{1000}{(1.02)^6}$$

$$P = \$887.96$$

5. What is the coupon on a 5-year bond trading at par? Assume annual coupon payments, face value of 1000 EUR and 3% interest rate.

$$P = \frac{C}{d} \cdot \left(1 - \frac{1}{(1+d)^n}\right) + \frac{VN}{(1+d)^n}$$

$$1000 = \frac{C}{0.03} \cdot \left(1 - \frac{1}{(1.03)^5}\right) + \frac{1000}{(1.03)^5}$$

$$1000 - \frac{1000}{(1.03)^5} = \frac{C}{0.03} \cdot \left(1 - \frac{1}{(1.03)^5}\right)$$

$$1000 \left(1 - \frac{1}{(1.03)^5}\right) = \frac{C}{0.03} \cdot \left(1 - \frac{1}{(1.03)^5}\right)$$

$$\frac{1000 \left(1 - \frac{1}{(1.03)^5}\right)}{\left(1 - \frac{1}{(1.03)^5}\right)} = \frac{C}{0.03} \cdot$$

$$1000 = \frac{C}{0.03}.$$

$$C = 30 \text{ EUR}$$

5.6.2 Applications

1. Suppose an investor holds a classic bond with the following characteristics:

   * The nominal value $800
   * 10% coupon rate
   * The coupon is paid annually, the maturity is 10 years
   * Interest rate: 5%; 6% and 8%

   What will be the price of the bond?

2. Let a classic bond with face value 1000 RON, coupon rate.

   * 10% and
   * 12%
   * 10% interest rate
   * Maturity 6, 4, 2 years, determine its price

3. Company A issued a bond with the following characteristics: face value 1200 EUR, coupon rate 4%, (coupon is paid annually), maturity 10 years, interest 5%, repayment being made at maturity.

   Company B issues a bond with a coupon rate of 8%, a maturity of 10 years, the nominal value 1000 EUR and the interest rate of 4%. What will investors prefer?

4. Suppose an investor holds a classic bond with the following characteristics:

   * The nominal value $1000.
   * 6% coupon rate.
   * The coupon is paid annually, the maturity is 5 years.
   * Interest rates are 3% in the first 2 years and 4% in the last two.

5. Suppose an investor holds a classic bond with the following characteristics:

   - The nominal value 2000 lei.
   - 8% coupon rate.
   - The coupon is paid annually, the maturity is 6 years.
   - Interest rates are 3%, 4%, 5%, 6%, 7%, and 8%, respectively.

6. What is the price of a zero-coupon bond with face value of 2000 EUR, evaluated for 12 years with interest rate of 6.5%?
7. What is the coupon on a 7-year bond trading at par? Assume annual coupon payments, face value of 3000 lei and 4.5% interest rate.

6

Portfolio Theory

6.1 One and Two-Stock Portfolios

Several shares will be listed on the market. Profitability of the stock i (R_i), in the time interval from $t = 0$ to $t = 1$, this time by the following formula:

$$R_i = \frac{(P_1 - P_0) + D_1}{P_0}$$

With P_0 and P_1 the course of the action was denoted at the moments $t = 0$, respectively $t = 1$, and with D_1 it was denoted the size of the dividend.

In the above formula the quantities P_1 and D_1 are random variables, which makes R_i random variable.

We will assume that for the future moment $t = 1$ a number of q possible states of the economy have been identified, as well as the probabilities p_k of achieving each state. In the identification of possible states will take into account the situation of the economic branch in which the company is issuing the stock i.

For each state k, based on the identification of P_{ik} rates and D_{ik} dividend will be calculated R_{ik} returns. In this way, the distribution is formed:

$$R_i : \begin{pmatrix} p_1 & p_2 & ,\ldots, & p_q \\ R_{i1} & R_{i2} & ,\ldots, & R_{iq} \end{pmatrix}$$

where $p_k \geq 0, k = \overline{1,q}$ and $\sum_{k=1}^{q} p_k = 1$.

The average return of stock i is:

$$E(R_i) = \sum_{k=1}^{q} p_k \cdot R_{ik}$$

And the variance is:

$$\sigma_i^2 = \text{var}(R_i) = E(R_i^2) - E(R_i)^2$$

where

$$E(R_i^2) = \sum_{k=1}^{q} p_k \cdot R_{ik}^2$$

According to the convention adopted in the financial-monetary field $\sigma_i = \sqrt{\text{var}(R_i)}$ quantifies the magnitude of the risk of stock i. The greater the magnitude of σ_i, the greater the risk assumed by an investor who buys the share i is. The above statement is valid only if the investor has managed to act and without introducing it into a portfolio in which there are other shares.

Definition
A vector $x = (x_1, x_2, \ldots, x_n)$ is called a_portfolio of n shares with $x_1 + x_2 + \ldots + x_n = 1$, where with $x_i, i = \overline{1,n}$ is denoted the share of the amount invested in share i in the total amount invested.

Observation
If market regulations allow short-selling operations, some of the components of vector x may be negative.

6.1.1 Risk and Return of a Portfolio

To write the equations of a portfolio, some of the properties will be recalled mean or variance of a random variable, respectively. They will be marked with the letter z random variables, and with the letter c will be denoted constants.

(a) Properties of the mean

$$E(c) = c$$
$$E(c \cdot z) = c \cdot E(z)$$
$$E(z_1 + z_2) = E(z_1) + E(z_2)$$

(b) Properties of the variance

$$\text{Var}(c) = 0$$
$$\text{Var}(c \cdot z) = c^2 \cdot E(z)$$
$$\text{Var}(z_1 + z_2) = \text{Var}(z_1) + \text{Var}(z_2) + 2 \cdot \sigma_1 \cdot \sigma_2 \cdot \rho_{12}$$

where ρ_{12} is the correlation coefficient between the two stocks and is calculated with the formula?

$$\rho_{12} = \frac{E\left[(z_1 - E(z_1))(z_2 - E(z_2))\right]}{\sigma_1 \cdot \sigma_2}.$$

The correlation coefficient ρ_{12} takes values between -1 and $+1$. If the value of ρ_{12} is close to 0, we say that the two stock are independent, but if the ρ_{12} is close to -1 or $+1$, we say that the two stocks are highly correlated.

From all the above, we can derive the formulas for the risk and the return of a two-stock portfolio. Assume that we have a two-stock portfolio $x = (x_1 x_2)$, $x_1 + x_2 = 1$. The two stocks $z1$ and $z2$ have the return and risks: $E(z_1)$, σ_1 and $E(z_2)$, σ_2 respectively. Then the return and risk of portfolio z could be computed as follows:

Return: $E(z) = x_1 \cdot E(z_1) + x_2 \cdot E(z_2)$
Risk: $\sigma_z^2 = x_1^2 \sigma_{z_1}^2 + x_2^2 \sigma_{z_2}^2 + 2 x_1 x_2 \sigma_{z_1}^2 \sigma_{z_2}^2 \rho_{12}$

Where ρ_{12} is the correlation coefficient between the stocks 1 and 2.

6.1.2 Solved Problems

1. We consider that two assets are listed on the market with returns $E(R_1) = E(R_2) = 0.1$ and risks $\sigma_1 = 0.15$, $\sigma_2 = 0.25$. The two assets evolve independently in the market, i.e., the correlation coefficient between the two assets is $\rho_{12} = 0$. Determine the covariance between the two assets and write the variance-covariance matrix.

Solution
We compute the covariance according to the formula: $\text{Cov}(R_1, R_2) = \sigma_{12} = \rho_{12} \sigma_1 \sigma_2 = 0$.

The variance-covariance matrix is: $\Omega = \begin{pmatrix} \sigma_1^2 & \sigma_{12} \\ \sigma_{12} & \sigma_2^2 \end{pmatrix} = \begin{pmatrix} 0.0225 & 0 \\ 0 & 0.0625 \end{pmatrix}$

2. We consider that two assets are listed on the market with returns $\mu = \begin{pmatrix} E(R_1) \\ E(R_2) \end{pmatrix} = \begin{pmatrix} 0.1 \\ 0.2 \end{pmatrix}$ and risks $\sigma_1 = 0.2$, $\sigma_2 = 0.3$. The correlation coefficient between the two assets is $\rho_{12} = -1$. Determine the covariance between the two assets and write the variance-covariance matrix.

Solution
We compute the covariance with the formula: $\sigma_{12} = \rho_{12} \sigma_1 \sigma_2 = (-1) \cdot 0.2 \cdot 0.3 = -0.06$.

The variance-covariance matrix is: $\Omega = \begin{pmatrix} 0.04 & -0.06 \\ -0.06 & 0.09 \end{pmatrix}$.

3. We consider a market stock (i). The return of stock (i), in the time range from $t = 0$ to $t = 1$, is denoted by (R_i) and has the following distribution:

$$R_i : \begin{pmatrix} 0.2 & 0.3 & 0.2 & 0.2 & 0.1 \\ 1.4 & 1.5 & 1.5 & 1.4 & 1.4 \end{pmatrix}.$$

The return of the stock is:

Solution
Return of the stock:

$$E(R_i) = \sum_{k=1}^{n} p_k \cdot R_{ik},$$ where p_k and R_k were previously defined.

Thus, we get:

$$E(R_i) = 0.2 \cdot 1.4 + 0.3 \cdot 1.5 + 0.2 \cdot 1.5 + 0.2 \cdot 1.4 + 0.1 \cdot 1.4$$

$$E(R_i) = 1.45$$

4. We consider an action (R_i) in the five possible future states:

$$R_i : \begin{pmatrix} 0.2 & 0.3 & 0.2 & 0.2 & 0.1 \\ 1.4 & 1.5 & 1.5 & 1.4 & 1.4 \end{pmatrix}$$

Compute the risk of the stock.

Solution

$$E(R_i^2) = \sum_{k=1}^{n} p_k \cdot R^2{}_k$$

$$E(R_i^2) = 0.2 \cdot 1.4^2 + 0.3 \cdot 1.5^2 + 0.2 \cdot 1.5^2 + 0.2 \cdot 1.4^2 + 0.1 \cdot 1.4^2$$

$$E(R_i^2) = 2.105$$

The variance is:

$$\sigma_i^2 = \text{var}(R_i) = E(R_i^2) - E(R_i)^2$$
$$= 2.105 - 1.45^2$$
$$= 2.105 - 1.45^2$$
$$= 2.105 - 2.1025$$
$$= 0.0025$$

The risk is: $\sigma_i = \sqrt{0.0025} = 0.05 = 5\%$

5. We consider a portfolio consisting of two shares R_1 and R_2. R_1 has the return $E(R_1) = 20\%$ and the risk $\sigma_1 = 8\%$, and R_2 it has the return $E(R_2) = 30\%$ and the risk $\sigma_2 = 9\%$. We consider a portfolio $w = (w_1, w_2)$, where w_1 and w_2 represents the portfolio weights of each share: $w_1 = 40\%$, $w_2 = 60\%$ and $\rho_{12} = -1$.

Compute the return of the portfolio.

Solution
We denote with R_p the portfolio obtained from the two actions. This portfolio consists of w_1 of the first stock and w_2 the second. Then:

$$R_p = w_1 \cdot R_1 + w_2 \cdot R_2$$

For this portfolio, we will compute the return:

$$E(R_p) = w_1 \cdot E(R_1) + w_2 \cdot E(R_2)$$

By plugging in the numbers, we get:

$$E(R_p) = w_1 \cdot 0.20 + w_2 \cdot 0.30$$
$$E(R_p) = 0.4 \cdot 0.2 + 0.6 \cdot 0.3$$
$$E(R_p) = 0.26$$
$$E(R_p) = 26\%$$

6. Compute the risk of the portfolio in the previous problem.

Solution

$$\sigma^2_{R_p} = (w_1)^2 \cdot \sigma_1^2 + (w_2)^2 \cdot \sigma_2^2 + 2(w_1)(w_2)\rho_{12}\sigma_1\sigma_2$$
$$\sigma^2_{R_p} = (0.4)^2 \cdot (0.08)^2 + (0.6)^2 \cdot (0.09)^2 + 2(0.4)(0.6)\rho_{12}(0.08)(0.09)$$
$$\sigma^2_{R_p} = 0.001024 + 0.002916 + 0.003456 \cdot \rho_{12}$$
$$\sigma^2_{R_p} = 0.00394 + 0.003456 \cdot (-1)$$
$$\sigma^2_{R_p} = 0.000484$$
$$\sigma_{R_p} = 0.022$$
$$\sigma_{R_p} = 2.2\%$$

6.1.3 Applications

1. We consider two assets on the market with given returns $E(R_1) = E(R_2) = 0.2$ and the risks $\sigma_1 = 0.1$, $\sigma_2 = 0.05$. The two assets evolve independently on the market, i.e., the correlation coefficient between the two assets is $\rho_{12} = 0$.

(a) Determine the covariance between the two assets.
(b) Determine the return and risk of the portfolio of shares with weights: 30% (w_1) and 70% (w_2).

2. We consider two assets on the market with given returns $E(R_1) = E(R_2) = 0.38$ and the risks $\sigma_1 = 0.12$, $\sigma_2 = 0.15$. The two assets evolve dependently on the market, and the correlation coefficient between the two assets is $\rho_{12} = 0.5$.

   (a) Determine the covariance between the two assets.
   (b) Determine the return and risk of the portfolio of shares with weights: 80% (w_1) and 20% (w_2).

3. We consider a market stock (i). The return of stock (i), in the time range from $t = 0$ to $t = 1$, is denoted by (R_i) and has the following distribution:

$$R_i : \begin{pmatrix} 0.25 & 0.15 & 0.4 & 0.1 & 0.1 \\ 1.2 & 0.15 & 1.3 & 1.4 & 1.5 \end{pmatrix}.$$

Calculate the average (expected) return and the risk of the stock.

4. We consider a market stock (i). The return of stock (i), in the time range from $t = 0$ to $t = 1$, is denoted by (R_i) and has the following distribution:

$$R_i : \begin{pmatrix} 0.1 & 0.2 & 0.1 & 0.3 & 0.3 \\ 2 & 2.2 & 2.3 & 2.4 & 2.5 \end{pmatrix}.$$

(a) Calculate the average (expected) return of the stock.
(b) Calculate the risk of the stock.

5. We consider two assets on the market with given returns $E(R_1) = 0.15$; $E(R_2) = 0.25$ and the risks $\sigma_1 = 0.04$; $\sigma_2 = 0.05$. The two assets evolve

independently on the market, i.e., the correlation coefficient between the two assets is $\rho_{12} = -0.75$.

(a) Determine the covariance between the two assets.
(b) Determine the return and risk of the portfolio of shares with weights: 65% (w_1) and 35% of (w_2).

Useful Formulas

$E(R_i) = \sum_{i=1}^{n} p_i \cdot x_i$; $E(R_i^2) = \sum_{i=1}^{n} p_i \cdot x_i^2$; $\sigma_i^2 = E(R_i^2) - [E(R_i)]^2$ (for pb 3 and 4).

If $R_p = w_1 R_1 + w_2 R_2$, then the return and risk are computed as follows (for pb 1 and 2):

$$E(R_p) = w_1 E(R_1) + w_2 E(R_2); \text{Cov}(R_1, R_2) = \sigma_1 \cdot \sigma_2 \cdot \rho_{12}$$

$$\sigma_p^2(R_p) = w_1^2 \sigma_1^2 + w_2^2 \sigma_2^2 + 2 w_1 \sigma_1 w_2 \sigma_2 \rho_{12}.$$

6.2 Three-Stock Portfolios

Now we will assume that we have a portfolio with three stocks. The three stocks z_1, z_2, and z_3 have the return and risks: $E(z_1)$, σ_1, $E(z_2)$, σ_2 and $E(z_3)$, σ_3 respectively. We also assume that ρ_{12} is the correlation coefficient between the stocks 1 and 2, ρ_{13} is the correlation coefficient between the stocks 1 and 3 and ρ_{23} is the correlation coefficient between the stocks 2 and 3.

We are able to derive the formulas for the risk and the return of a three-stock portfolio. Assume that we have a two-stock portfolio $x = (x_1, x_2, x_3)$, $x_1 + x_2 + x_3 = 1$. Then the return and risk of portfolio z could be computed as follows:

Return: $E(z) = x_1 \cdot E(z_1) + x_2 \cdot E(z_2) + x_3 \cdot E(z_3)$

Risk: $\sigma_z^2 = x_1^2 \sigma_{z_1}^2 + x_2^2 \sigma_{z_2}^2 + x_3^2 \sigma_{z_3}^2 + 2 x_1 x_2 \sigma_{z_1} \sigma_{z_2} \rho_{12} + 2 x_1 x_3 \sigma_{z_1} \sigma_{z_3} \rho_{13}$
$\quad + 2 x_2 x_3 \sigma_{z_2} \sigma_{z_3} \rho_{23}$

6.2.1 Solved Problems

1. We consider a three-stock portfolio with the following weights: $w_1 = 50\%$, $w_2 = 30\%$, $w_3 = 20\%$. The returns of the three stocks are: $E(R_1) = 12\%$, $E(R_1) = 14\%$, $E(R_3) = 16\%$. Compute the return of the portfolio.

Solution
We have: $w^T = (0.5; 0.3; 0.2)$.
The return of the portfolio is:

$$E(R_p) = w_1 \cdot E(R_1) + w_2 \cdot E(R_2) + w_3 \cdot E(R_3)$$

By plugging in the numbers, we get:

$$E(R_p) = (0.5) \cdot 0.12 + (0.3) \cdot 0.14 + (0.2) \cdot 0.16$$

$$E(R_p) = 0.134$$

2. We will consider a three-stock portfolio. The returns of the three stocks are: $E(R_1) = 16\%$, $E(R_2) = 18\%$, $E(R_2) = 20\%$. The risks are: $\sigma_1 = 10\%$, $\sigma_2 = 15\%$ and $\sigma_3 = 18\%$. Correlation coefficients are: $\rho_{12} = 0.20$, $\rho_{23} = -0.25$ and $\rho_{13} = 0$.

Consider a portfolio with the following structure: $x_1 = 30\%$, $x_2 = 30\%$, $x_3 = 40\%$ (weights).
Determine:

(a) Variance-covariance matrix Ω
(b) Expected return of the portfolio $E(R_p)$
(c) Risk of the portfolio σ_p

Solution
(a) We will start with computing the covariances:

$$\sigma_{12} = \rho_{12} \cdot \sigma_1 \cdot \sigma_2 = 0.2 \cdot 0.1 \cdot 0.15 = 0.003$$

$$\sigma_{13} = \rho_{13} \cdot \sigma_1 \cdot \sigma_3 = 0 \cdot 0.1 \cdot 0.18 = 0$$

$$\sigma_{23} = \rho_{23} \cdot \sigma_2 \cdot \sigma_3 = -0.25 \cdot 0.15 \cdot 0.18 = -0.00675$$

The variance-covariance matrix is:

$$\Omega = \begin{pmatrix} \sigma_{11} & \sigma_{12} & \sigma_{13} \\ \sigma_{21} & \sigma_{22} & \sigma_{23} \\ \sigma_{31} & \sigma_{32} & \sigma_{33} \end{pmatrix}.$$

Given that $\sigma_{ii} = \sigma^2_i$ and $\sigma_{ij} = \sigma_{ij}$ for any $i, j = \overline{1,3}$, we get:

$$\Omega = \begin{pmatrix} (0.1)^2 & 0.003 & 0 \\ 0.003 & (0.15)^2 & -0.00675 \\ 0 & -0.00675 & (0.18)^2 \end{pmatrix}$$

From this, we get:

$$\Omega = \begin{pmatrix} 0.01 & 0.003 & 0 \\ 0.003 & 0.0225 & -0.00675 \\ 0 & -0.00675 & 0.0324 \end{pmatrix}$$

(b) Portfolio has the following structure: $x_1 = 30\%$, $x_2 = 30\%$, $x_3 = 40\%$, which means: $x^T = (0.3; 0.3; 0.4)$.

Thus, the expected return of the portfolio is:

$$E(R_p) = x_1 \cdot E(R_1) + x_2 \cdot E(R_2) + x_3 \cdot E(R_3)$$

By plugging in the given values, we get:

$$E(R_p) = (0.3) \cdot 0.16 + (0.3) \cdot 0.18 + (0.4) \cdot 0.2$$

$$E(R_p) = 0.182$$

(c) The variance of the portfolio is:

$$\sigma_p^2 = x^T \cdot \Omega \cdot x$$

$$= (0.3; 0.3; 0.4) \begin{pmatrix} 0.01 & 0.003 & 0 \\ 0.003 & 0.0225 & -0.00675 \\ 0 & -0.00675 & 0.0324 \end{pmatrix} \begin{pmatrix} 0.3 \\ 0.3 \\ 0.4 \end{pmatrix}$$

$$= (0.3; 0.3; 0.4) \begin{pmatrix} 0.0039 \\ 0.00495 \\ 0.0110 \end{pmatrix}$$

$$= 0.3 \cdot 0.0039 + 0.3 \cdot 0.0045 + 0.4 \cdot 0.011$$

$$= 0.00692$$

$$\sigma_p = 0.0832$$

Thus, we could conclude that the portfolio has a return of 18.2% and risk 8.32%.

3. We will consider a three-stock portfolio. The returns of the three stocks are: $E(R_1) = 10\%$, $E(R_2) = 8\%$, $E(R_2) = 12\%$. The risks are: $\sigma_1 = 2\%$, $\sigma_2 = 5\%$, $\sigma_3 = 3\%$. Correlation coefficients are: $\rho_{12} = 0$, $\rho_{23} = -0.25$ and $\rho_{13} = +0.75$.

Consider a portfolio with the following structure: $x_1 = 20\%$, $x_2 = 30\%$, $x_3 = 50\%$ (weights).

Determine the expected return and the risk of the portfolio.

Solution

$$E(R_p) = (0.2) \cdot 0.1 + (0.3) \cdot 0.08 + (0.5) \cdot 0.12 = 0.104$$

$$\sigma_p^2 = w_1^2\sigma_1^2 + w_2^2\sigma_2^2 + w_3^2\sigma_3^2 + 2w_1\sigma_1 w_2\sigma_2\rho_{12} + 2w_2\sigma_2 w_3\sigma_3\rho_{23} + 2w_1\sigma_1 w_3\sigma_3\rho_{13}$$

$$\sigma_p^2 = 0.2^2 0.022^2 + 0.3^2 0.05^2 + 0.5^2 0.03^2 + 2(0.2)(0.02)(0.3)(0.05)(0)$$
$$+ 2(0.2)(0.02)(0.5)(0.03)(0.75) + 2(0.3)(0.05)(0.5)(0.03)(-0.25)$$

$$\sigma_p^2 = 0.0004435$$

$$\sigma_p = 0.0210594$$

Risk is 2.1% and return is 10.4%.

6.2.2 Applications

4. We will consider a three-stock portfolio. The returns of the three stocks are: $E(R_1) = 12\%$, $E(R_2) = 10\%$, $E(R_2) = 14\%$. The risks are: $\sigma_1 = 4\%$, $\sigma_2 = 5\%$ and $\sigma_3 = 6\%$. Correlation coefficients are: $\rho_{12} = -0.20$, $\rho_{23} = 0$ and $\rho_{13} = +0.5$.
Consider a portfolio with the following structure: $x_1 = 40\%$, $x_2 = 40\%$, $x_3 = 20\%$ (weights).
Determine the expected return and the risk of the portfolio.

5. We will consider a three-stock portfolio. The returns of the three stocks are: $E(R_1) = 18\%$, $E(R_2) = 16\%$, $E(R_2) = 14\%$. The risks are: $\sigma_1 = 8\%$, $\sigma_2 = 6\%$ and $\sigma_3 = 4\%$. Correlation coefficients are: $\rho_{12} = 0.20$, $\rho_{23} = -0.25$ and $\rho_{13} = -0.6$.
Consider a portfolio with the following structure: $x_1 = 30\%$, $x_2 = 30\%$, $x_3 = 40\%$ (weights).
Determine the expected return and the risk of the portfolio.

6. We will consider a three-stock portfolio. The returns of the three stocks are: $E(R_1) = 14\%$, $E(R_2) = 9\%$, $E(R_2) = 10\%$. The risks are: $\sigma_1 = 7\%$, $\sigma_2 = 4\%$ and $\sigma_3 = 6\%$. Correlation coefficients are: $\rho_{12} = -0.4$, $\rho_{23} = +0.4$ and $\rho_{13} = 0$.
Consider a portfolio with the following structure: $x_1 = 40\%$, $x_2 = 40\%$, $x_3 = 20\%$ (weights).
Determine the expected return and the risk of the portfolio.

Useful Formulas
Return of the portfolio:

$$E(R_p) = w_1 E(R_1) + w_2 E(R_2) + w_3 E(R_3).$$

Risk of the portfolio:

$$\sigma_p^2 = w_1^2 \sigma_1^2 + w_2^2 \sigma_2^2 + w_3^2 \sigma_3^2 + 2w_1 \sigma_1 w_2 \sigma_2 \rho_{12} + 2w_2 \sigma_2 w_3 \sigma_3 \rho_{23} + 2w_1 \sigma_1 w_3 \sigma_3 \rho_{13} \text{ or}$$

$$\sigma_p^2 = x^T \cdot \Omega \cdot x$$

Variance-covariance matrix:

$$\Omega = \begin{pmatrix} \sigma_{11} & \sigma_{12} & \sigma_{13} \\ \sigma_{21} & \sigma_{22} & \sigma_{23} \\ \sigma_{31} & \sigma_{32} & \sigma_{33} \end{pmatrix}; \sigma_{ii} = \sigma_i^2, \text{ and } \sigma_{ij} = \sigma_{ji} \text{ for any } i, j = \overline{1,3},$$

$$\sigma_{ij} = \sigma_i \cdot \sigma_j \cdot \rho_{ij}$$

6.3 Efficient Portfolios Consisting of Two Risky Assets

In this section, for a portfolio of two shares, we want to find out how could we choose the weights such that the risk of the portfolio is minimum for a fixed return or how to maximize the return, when the risk is fixed.

We will analyze each case separately.

6.3.1 Minimum Risk for a Fixed Return

Suppose we have a portfolio with two stocks (w_1, w_2), where $w_1 + w_2 = 1$.

For each stock, the risk and return were calculated: $E(z_1)$, σ_1 and $E(z_2)$, σ_2, respectively.

The question we want to answer is: What are the weights w1 and w2 so that the risk is minimum for a fixed return?

For a two-stock portfolio, with two stocks z_1 and z_2 we have the return and risks: The correlation coefficient is ρ_{12}. The risk and return of the portfolio is:

Return: $E(z) = x_1 \cdot E(z_1) + x_2 \cdot E(z_2)$
Risk: $\sigma_z^2 = x_1^2 \sigma_{z_1}^2 + x_2^2 \sigma_{z_2}^2 + 2x_1 x_2 \sigma_{z_1}^2 \sigma_{z_2}^2 \rho_{12}$

Given that the sum of the weights is 1, we substitute back and get:
Expected return: $E(R_P) = w_1 E(R_1) + (1 - w_1) E(R_2)$
Variance: $s_P^2 = w_1^2 s_1^2 + (1 - w_1)^2 s_2^2 + 2w_1(1 - w_1) s_{12}$

$$s_P^2 = w_1^2 s_1^2 + (1-w_1)^2 s_2^2 + 2w_1(1-w_1)(\rho s_1 s_2)$$

s_P^2 is minimum when:

$$\frac{\partial \sigma_P}{\partial W_1} = 0 \text{ and } \frac{\partial^2 \sigma_P^2}{\partial w_1^2} > 0$$

Risk is:

$$s_P^2 = w_1^2 s_1^2 + (1-w_1)^2 s_2^2 + 2w_1(1-w_1)(\rho s_1 s_2)$$
$$s_P^2 = w_1^2 s_1^2 + w_1^2 s_2^2 - 2w_1 s_2^2 + s_2^2 + 2w_1(1-w_1)(\rho s_1 s_2)$$
$$s_P^2 = w_1^2 (s_1^2 + s_2^2 - 2\rho s_1 s_2) - 2(s_2^2 + \rho s_1 s_2) W_1 + s_2^2$$

s_P^2 is minimum when:

$$2w_1 (s_1^2 + s_2^2 - 2\rho s_1 s_2) - 2(s_2^2 + \rho s_1 s_2) = 0 \mid : 2$$

$$w_1\left(s_1^2 + s_2^2 - 2\rho s_1 s_2\right) = s_2^2 + \rho s_1 s_2$$

$$w_1 = \frac{\sigma_2^2 + \rho \cdot \sigma_1 \cdot \sigma_2}{\sigma_1^2 + \sigma_2^2 - 2\rho \cdot \sigma_1 \cdot \sigma_2}$$

6.3.2 Solved Problems

1. Consider a portfolio with two stocks with returns $\mu = \begin{pmatrix} E(R_1) \\ E(R_2) \end{pmatrix} = \begin{pmatrix} 0.3 \\ 0.4 \end{pmatrix}$ and risks $\sigma_1 = 0.1$, $\sigma_2 = 0.2$ and $\rho_{12} = 0$. Consider a portfolio P with the weights $x = \begin{pmatrix} x_1 \\ x_2 \end{pmatrix}$ with $x_2 = 1 - x_1$.

   (a) What are the return and risk of the portfolio?
   (b) Out of all portfolios determined in point a), determine the one with the minimum risk. Calculate its structure, risk, and return.

Solution
(a) $E(R_x) = x_1 E(R_1) + x_2 E(R_2) = 0.3x_1 + 0.4x_2 = 0.3x_1 + 0.4(1 - x_1)$
$= -0.1$

$x_1 + 0.4 \ \sigma^2{}_p = x_1^2 \sigma_1^2 + x_2^2 \sigma_2^2 + 2x_1 x_2 \sigma_{12} = 0.01 x_1^2 + 0.04(1 - x_1)^2 + 2 \cdot 0$
$= 0.05 x_1^2 - 0.08 x_1 + 0.04$

(b) We are minimizing the variance of portfolio P:

$$\min \sigma_P^2 = \frac{\partial \sigma_P^2}{\partial x_1} = 0 \Rightarrow 0.1 x_1 - 0.08 = 0 \Rightarrow x_1 = 0.8 \Rightarrow x_2 = 0.2$$

Hence, the portfolio has minimum risk if the weights are 80% and 20%.

$$x = \begin{pmatrix} 0.8 \\ 0.2 \end{pmatrix}$$

Thus, the return of the portfolio is:

$$E(R_x) = -0.1x_1 + 0.4 = -0.1(0.8) + 0.4 = 0.32$$
$$E(R_x) = 32\%$$

The variance is computed using the formula:

$$\sigma^2_p = 0.05x_1^2 - 0.08x_1 + 0.04 = 0.05(0.8)^2 - 0.08(0.8) + 0.04 = 0.008$$
$$\sigma_p = 8.94\%$$

2. Consider a portfolio with two stocks with returns $\mu = \begin{pmatrix} E(R_1) \\ E(R_2) \end{pmatrix} = \begin{pmatrix} 0.10 \\ 0.17 \end{pmatrix}$ and risks $\sigma_1 = 0.25$, $\sigma_2 = 0.35$ and $\rho_{12} = -1$. Consider a portfolio P with the weights $x = \begin{pmatrix} x_1 \\ x_2 \end{pmatrix}$ with $x_2 = 1 - x_1$.

   (a) What are the return and risk of the portfolio?
   (b) Out of all portfolios determined at a), determine the one with the minimum risk. Calculate its structure, risk, and return.

Solution
(a) $E(R_x) = x_1 E(R_1) + x_2 E(R_2) = 0.10x_1 + 0.17x_2 = 0.10x_1 + 0.17(1 - x_1)$
   $= -0.07x_1 + 0.17$

$\sigma^2_p = x_1^2\sigma_1^2 + x_2^2\sigma_2^2 + 2x_1 x_2 \rho_{12}\sigma_1\sigma_2 = 0.0625x_1^2 + 0.1225(1-x_1)^2$
$+ 2(-1)0.25 \cdot 0.35 \cdot x_1(1-x_1) = 0.36x_1^2 - 0.42x_1 + 0.1225$

(b) We are minimizing the variance of portfolio P:

$$\min \sigma_P^2 = \frac{\partial \sigma_P^2}{\partial x_1} = 0 \Rightarrow 0.72 x_1 - 0.42 = 0 \Rightarrow x_1 = 0.5833 \Rightarrow x_2 = 0.4167$$

Hence, the portfolio has minimum risk if the weights are 58.33% and 41.67%.

$$x = \begin{pmatrix} 0.5833 \\ 0.4167 \end{pmatrix}$$

Thus, the return of the portfolio is:

$$E(R_x) = -0.07 x_1 + 0.17 = -0.07 \cdot 0.5833 + 0.17 = 0.129$$

The variance is computed using the formula:

$$\sigma_p^2 = 0.36 x_1^2 - 0.42 x_1 + 0.1225 = 0.36 \cdot 0.5833^2 - 0.42 \cdot 0.5833 + 0.1225 = 0$$

Observation

If the correlation coefficient of a two-stock portfolio is -1, then the risk of the portfolio is 0.

3. Consider a portfolio with two stocks with returns $\mu = \begin{pmatrix} E(R_1) \\ E(R_2) \end{pmatrix} = \begin{pmatrix} 0.12 \\ 0.14 \end{pmatrix}$ and risks $\sigma_1 = 0.02$, $\sigma_2 = 0.05$ and $\rho_{12} = +0.2$. Consider a portfolio P with the weights $x = \begin{pmatrix} x_1 \\ x_2 \end{pmatrix}$ with $x_2 = 1 - x_1$.

(a) What are the return and risk of the portfolio?
(b) Out of all portfolios determined in point a), find the one with the minimum risk. Calculate its structure, risk, and return.

4. Consider a portfolio with two stocks with returns $\mu = \begin{pmatrix} E(R_1) \\ E(R_2) \end{pmatrix} = \begin{pmatrix} 0.16 \\ 0.18 \end{pmatrix}$ and risks $\sigma_1 = 0.05$, $\sigma_2 = 0.04$ and

$\rho_{12} = -0.5$. Consider a portfolio P with the weights $x = \begin{pmatrix} x_1 \\ x_2 \end{pmatrix}$ with $x_2 = 1 - x_1$.

(a) What are the return and risk of the portfolio?
(b) Of all the P portfolios determined in point a), determine the one with the minimum risk. Calculate its structure, risk, and return.

6.3.3 Maximum Return

Again, we will consider a two-stock portfolio $w = (w_1, w_2)$. For each stock, the risk and return were calculated: $E(z_1)$, σ_1 and $E(z_2)$, σ_2, respectively.
The risk and return are:

$$E(R_P) = w_1 E(R_1) + (1 - w_1) E(R_2)$$
$$s^2{}_P = w^2{}_1 s^2{}_1 + (1 - w_1)^2 s^2{}_2 + 2w_1(1 - w_1) s_{12}$$
$$s^2{}_P = w^2{}_1 s^2{}_1 + (1 - w_1)^2 s^2{}_2 + 2w_1(1 - w_1)(\rho s_1 s_2)$$

Assume that $s^2{}_P$ is fixed: $s^2{}_P = a$.
Hence, we get

$$w^2{}_1 s^2{}_1 + (1 - w_1)^2 s^2{}_2 + 2w_1(1 - w_1)(\rho s_1 s_2) - a = 0$$

Now we will solve the quadratic equation, using the formula:

$$x_{1,2} = \frac{-b \pm \sqrt{\Delta}}{2a}$$

We solve the quadratic equation and consider the positive value, the value for which the maximum return is calculated.

$$E(R_p) = w_1 E(R_1) + (1-w_1) E(R_2)$$

6.3.4 Solved Problems

5. Consider a portfolio with two stocks with returns
$$\mu = \begin{pmatrix} E(R_1) \\ E(R_2) \end{pmatrix} = \begin{pmatrix} 0.10 \\ 0.17 \end{pmatrix} \text{ and risks } \sigma_1 = 0.25, \quad \sigma_2 = 0.35 \text{ and } \rho_{12} = -1.$$
Consider a portfolio P with the weights $x = \begin{pmatrix} x_1 \\ x_2 \end{pmatrix}$ with $x_2 = 1 - x_1$.

(a) What are the return and risk of the portfolio?
(b) Out of all the P portfolios determined in point a), determine the one with maximum return and variance of 50%.

Solution

a) $E(R_x) = x_1 E(R_1) + x_2 E(R_2) = 0.10 x_1 + 0.17 x_2$
$= 0.10 x_1 + 0.17(1 - x_1) = -0.07 x_1 + 0.17$

$\sigma^2_p = x_1^2 \sigma_1^2 + x_2^2 \sigma_2^2 + 2 x_1 x_2 \sigma_{12} = 0.0625 x_1^2 + 0.1225(1 - x_1)^2$
$+ 2 \cdot (-0.0875) x_1 (1 - x_1)$
$= 0.36 x_1^2 - 0.42 x_1 + 0.1225$

b) $0.36 x_1^2 - 0.42 x_1 + 0.1225 = 0.5$

$0.36 x_1^2 - 0.42 x_1 - 0.3775 = 0$

Using the quadratic formula, we get:

$$\Delta = b^2 - 4ac = (0.42)^2 - 4(0.36)(-0.3775)$$

$$x_{1,2} = \frac{-b \pm \sqrt{\Delta}}{2a}$$

The solutions are: $x_{1,1} = 0.96$ and $x_{1,2} = 0.21$.
Now we compute the expected return:

$E(R_{x_{1,1}}) = -0.07(0.96) + 0.17 = 0.1028$ and $E(R_{x_{1,2}}) = -0.07(0.21) + 0.17 = 0.1553$.

Since $E(R_{x_{11}}) < E(R_{x_{12}})$, we conclude that maximum return of the portfolio is 15.53%.

6.3.5 Applications

1. Consider a portfolio with two stocks with returns $\mu = \begin{pmatrix} E(R_1) \\ E(R_2) \end{pmatrix} = \begin{pmatrix} 0.3 \\ 0.4 \end{pmatrix}$

   and risks $\sigma_1 = 0.1$, $\sigma_2 = 0.2$ and $\rho_{12} = 0$. Consider a portfolio P with the weights $x = \begin{pmatrix} x_1 \\ x_2 \end{pmatrix}$ with $x_2 = 1 - x_1$.

   (a) What are the return and risk of the portfolio?
   (b) Out of all portfolios determined in point a), determine the portfolio with maximum return for a given variance of 4.5%.

2. Consider a portfolio with two stocks with returns

   $\mu = \begin{pmatrix} E(R_1) \\ E(R_2) \end{pmatrix} = \begin{pmatrix} 0.15 \\ 0.12 \end{pmatrix}$ and risks $\sigma_1 = 0.01$, $\sigma_2 = 0.03$ and

   $\rho_{12} = +0.75$. Consider a portfolio P with the weights $x = \begin{pmatrix} x_1 \\ x_2 \end{pmatrix}$ with

   $x_2 = 1 - x_1$.

   (a) What are the return and risk of the portfolio?
   (b) Of all the P portfolios determined in point a), determine the portfolio with maximum return for a given variance of 4%.

3. Consider a portfolio with two stocks with returns

   $\mu = \begin{pmatrix} E(R_1) \\ E(R_2) \end{pmatrix} = \begin{pmatrix} 0.11 \\ 0.12 \end{pmatrix}$ and risks $\sigma_1 = 0.02$, $\sigma_2 = 0.05$ and

   $\rho_{12} = -0.25$.

   Consider a portfolio P with the weights $x = \begin{pmatrix} x_1 \\ x_2 \end{pmatrix}$ with $x_2 = 1 - x_1$.

(a) What are the return and risk of the portfolio?
(b) Of all the P portfolios determined in point a), determine the portfolio with maximum return for a given risk of 3%.

Useful Formulas

$$E(R_p) = w_1 E(R_1) + w_2 E(R_2);$$

$$\sigma_p^2(R_p) = w_1^2 \sigma_1^2 + w_2^2 \sigma_2^2 + 2 w_1 \sigma_1 w_2 \sigma_2 \rho_{12}$$

Finding the roots of a quadratic equation.

$$\Delta = b^2 - 4ac;$$

$$x_{1,2} = \frac{-b \pm \sqrt{\Delta}}{2a}$$

7

Derivatives

The markets that have been presented so far are markets in which spot transactions are performed, respectively, the change of ownership of a financial security for an amount of money takes place immediately, referred to it as "spot" financial market. However, an alternative market has emerged in which transactions are carried out considering different "rights" associated with financial securities. Instruments traded on such a market are called financial instruments derivatives.

Derivatives instruments or derivatives are financial instruments whose values depend on or derives from the value of another instrument, called the support asset. The support assets can be represented by commodities, stocks, interest rate, exchange rate, stock indices, etc.

Derivatives have emerged in response to the needs of the commodity market. The main requirement that derivatives must meet is the management or control of a specific risk, which may occur over a period of time. Those who trade in goods for commercial purposes are faced with the requirement to reach a compromise between:

- A long-term contract for the delivery of goods, which often provides for a strictly fixed price but a variable quantity (above a certain quantity minimum).
- The purchase of the respective good during the contract at the market price, a price that can vary significantly from a period to other.

Take the example of a flour producer who wants to negotiate a significant number of sales contracts at a fixed price with different producers of bakery products. The contracts will run for 12 months and will take effect in 4 months. Wheat production will be obtained, however, after 2 months, its volume not being known at the time of concluding the contract. The quantities to be delivered are estimated above a certain fixed minimum quantity monthly.

The flour producer cannot negotiate on the basis of the previous or current price because:

- This year's harvest could be either at a better level or at a lower level or at a level equivalent to that of this previous year.
- Demand for wheat could be much higher or lower compared to the previous year.
- Wheat production in other countries can be at significantly different levels, thus influencing the price of wheat at world.

Each of these factors can cause a considerable change in the price of wheat in the coming year. This variation may be in favor of the provider, but the risk involved in the operation is too great to be ignored. If the demand is much higher than the supply, it is possible that the entire required quantity can only be obtained at a certain price. The flour producer is interested in being able to set a fixed level of the quantity of wheat he will buy and the price at which it is to be sold.

If the producer does not want to negotiate the contract based on an estimated price, he may try to estimate the quantity of wheat he needs, buy it now and store it until requested. However, trying to buy a large amount of wheat at the end of the season could significantly raise prices. On the other hand, payment must be made immediately and the operation of storing the goods involves certain costs.

Another possibility would be to use a derivative instrument to reduce or avoid the risk. A financial derivative product has a value derived from the value of the underlying asset. In this way, the risk involved in the physical provision of the respective asset is separated from the provision of the derivative financial product. In such cases, it is said that the derivative product is an insurance against the risk, or that the risk has been covered. There are three possibilities for managing price risks and amount:

1. A forward contract is an agreement to sell/buy a quantity of an asset, at a predetermined price, within a specified future time (either on a fixed date or within a certain time frame). This contract is not a derivative in the true sense of the word, but we present it here to make a difference to a derivative product itself.
2. A futures contract is an agreement to sell/buy a standard quantity of an asset at market price for futures contracts at a certain time in future.
3. The option contract represents the right (but not the obligation) to sell/buy a quantity of an asset at a certain price, at a certain date in the future (either specified or at choice, depending on the clauses contract).

Obviously, each of these solutions involves a cost, which could become higher than the cost of the situation in which no action is taken, and the market price is paid from the moment the purchase of the goods is made. However, if the price of the derivative is not exaggerated, for the vast majority of transactions, it is a cost worth taking.

Companies that buy goods, process them and then sell the resulting products, make a profit from the value added that results from the processing action. Therefore, these companies are not very interested in the current purchase price of the underlying asset, so much time. So, those companies prefer to accept the payment of a premium (linked to a derivative transaction) to have the security of a certain price and a certain quantity.

Theoretically, derivatives can be used for any transaction that will take place in the future and in which either the price or the quantity are uncertain. In practice, however, a restriction has been imposed, namely that only certain categories/types of securities are traded on derivatives markets. active.

When a derivative contract is concluded, the risk does not go away. The issuer accepts the risk in exchange for the price of the derivative instrument. The issuer may accept the risk as a speculative transaction, but it is more likely that it is a component of an intermediary transaction. In other words, the issuer relies on many derivative contracts that are offset against each other, at least partial.

Net risk is considerably lower than most accepted individual risks. The net position can be covered by other issuers. For this, there must be an active market for derivatives, based on important transactions with certain specific assets. Therefore, there are markets for commodity derivatives for goods (wheat, copper, cocoa, tea, coffee, oil, etc.), for major currencies and for certain securities. Value.

In addition to the risk transfer function mentioned above, derivatives markets provide another very important function–pricing. Those who trade in these markets are concerned about the accuracy of pricing and their likely trend in the future. Therefore, the understanding of price trends for different derivatives will reflect market estimates of the future evolution of prices.

These predictions may not be very accurate (this is the idea behind speculators); however, they are generally based on specialized analyzes that may not be accessible to all investors. The price of the derivative instrument is influenced by the demand for it, reflecting any reduction or increase in the volume of transactions with the underlying asset.

Viewed through the prism of the main objective, the derivatives market is similar to that of insurance, risk management being the main motivation for the existence of the insurance market. Another similarity is that the price of a derivative is called a premium, as in the case of insurance contracts. The similarity with insurance is not perfect, as insurance risks are not traded by individual investors in the market in the same way that financial derivatives are traded.

Like securities and derivatives, derivatives can be traded on either an organized market (on the stock exchange) or the over-the-counter (OTC) market. Thus, in the case of trading on the stock markets, standardized contracts are concluded, which have as standard elements: the underlying asset, the size of the contract, the maturity date, the price variation step, the execution of the contract, etc. For example, coffee-based derivatives are traded in five tone lots, while US government bond derivatives are traded in batches with a face value of $ 100,000. The main advantage of using standard contracts is that they can be traded faster and are longer liquids.

In addition, the transactions are carried out through the clearing house, which is the intermediary of the exchange, so that the buyer and the seller do not know each other. Trading on stock exchanges has the advantage of observing strict rules by all participants, in case of non-fulfillment of obligations involving the clearing house. Thus, the stock market gives security to those who trade in terms of trading partners: to those who sell the securities that they will receive money, and to those who invest that they will receive the securities for advanced funds. The instruments traded are futures contracts and options.

Because the stock exchange establishes its own rules of operation, it is best able to ensure the financial capacity of those who trade within it (members of the stock exchange). The stock exchange/clearing house does not engage in operations on its own account, so that each transaction is made by debiting/crediting the accounts of the seller, respectively the buyer. Investors may not place sell/purchase orders directly on the stock exchange, but only through a member (broker), who will charge a commission for the provision of this service.

The largest stock exchanges in the world that trade derivatives are the Chicago Mercantile Exchange (CME) and the Chicago Board of Trade (CBT), followed by the London International Financial Futures Exchange (LIFFE). The existing system for all these exchanges is direct trading between brokers, and the London Stock Exchange also uses, at the end of the day, trading. Electronics.

In the case of OTC trading, contracts are concluded by direct negotiation between partners, therefore they are non-standardized contracts.

Trading on the OTC market has advantages such as

* The transaction can be concluded for any quantity and with any due date, in accordance with the requirements the client.
* Prices are to a lesser extent influenced by the volume of transactions made with a particular instrument derived.

Disadvantages of OTC transactions include

- Contracts are more expensive.
- Because the terms of the contract are not standardized, it is difficult to sell the contracts on the market secondary.
- The conditions imposed by the partner (often a major bank) may be restrictive.
- It is difficult to verify the accuracy of the process of establishing prices.

The most important component of the OTC derivatives market is transactions on currency.

There are three main types of operators in this market, each with a specific role.

1. Hedger traders try to eliminate or reduce the risk associated with regular transactions. To do this, they need partners who are willing, through market transactions, to take over the risk.
2. Speculators–act as a partner in most hedging operations. They are not interested in owning a particular asset but aim to make a profit from the positions they take in the market on various assets. Positions can be filled for a very short time (a few minutes), for a day, or for a longer period long.
3. Arbitrators monitor the prices of derivatives in several markets and aim to make a profit "by buying cheap and selling expensive" in these markets. By doing so, they help to reduce the differences in prices in these markets, increasing the correlation between markets.

The most frequently traded instruments on the OTC markets are *forward, swap, and options.*

7.1 Options

The option is a standardized contract that gives the buyer the right, but not the obligation, to buy or sell the underlying asset at a predetermined price (exercise price) against a paid amount. Seller (first) to completion contract, a period default.

The options can be of two types: *standardized and non-standardized* (traditional, conventional). option non-standard (traditional, conventional). The non-standardized option is the most frequently used and it was created to meet the buyer's quantity, price, and delivery requirements; therefore, these options are not traded on the secondary market.

Depending on how you exercise, there are two categories of options:

* The *European option* can only be exercised on a certain date, specified in the contract.
* The *American option* may be exercised at any time until the expiration of the contract.

These names are not related to the location of the option contracts, as both types of options are available in both Europe and the Americas. Obviously, American-style options are more expensive than European-type options.

The options can be: buy *(call option) or sell (put option)*. The rights conferred by the option contracts are obtained in exchange for a premium (the price of the option), which reflects the risk assumed by the issuer option.

Depending on the evolution of the underlying asset price, the options are:

* At-the-money, in which case the exercise price equals the price of the underlying asset.
* In-the-money, the contract is exercised, for a call option if the exchange rate of the underlying asset is higher than the exercise price, and for an option put if the exchange rate of the underlying asset is lower than the of exercise.

- Out-the-money, if the contract is not exercised, so the value of the option payoff is zero, for a call option when the exchange rate of the underlying asset is lower than the exercise value, and for the, when the price of the underlying asset is higher than exercise.

Options are available for commodities, stocks, bonds, interest rates and currencies. They are widely used as hedging instruments but can also be used for speculative operations. However, speculators on derivatives usually prefer to do so these process with contracts futures, because are May cheap.

7.2 Standardized Options

A standardized option is a contract through which a standard volume of the underlying asset is traded through the stock exchange. The expiration date of the option—the contract—is set, but the option can be sold or exercised at any time; thus, the American/European option distinction is irrelevant. The value of the option varies with the change in the price of the underlying asset, and may also have value 0.

The features of a standardized option are:

- The quantities traded are standardized.
- The price is not a continuous variable, there is a minimum variation that must be observed—for example, in the USA the exercise price is a multiple of 2.50 USD.
- The expiry dates of the option are set in three cycles over a year—the first being January, April, July, October, the second February, May, August, November and the third March, June, September, and December—each option has a duration of 3, 6, or 9 months.
- When an option is sold, three exercise prices are offered for each cycle.
- Trading costs are lower than in the case of a non-standard option; trades on a very secondary market liquidate.
- There is no risk to the transaction partner because all transactions are conducted through a clearing.
- Significant transaction prices are given advertising.

Most standardized options traded are based on the assets of major companies. However, other types of standardized options are traded, of which we mention:

- Index options of the markets in which they are traded actions
- Three-month interest rate options on deposits in Eurodollars
- Three-month interest rate options on deposits in euro
- Options on maturing treasury bills distant
- Options on treasury bills issued by the governments of foreign countries (USA, the main European states developed)
- Contract options futures

Futures options have appeared relatively recently and are a necessary tool in the development of the international financial system. By purchasing an option on futures contracts, the beneficiary has the right (but not the obligation) to perform hedging/speculative operations. If the option is exercised, the cost of the hedging transaction includes both the cost of the futures contract and the cost of the option contract; if the option is not exercised, the cost incurred will only be the cost of the option. The latter case assumes that the sight rate is better and the beneficiary makes a profit.

Investors will buy options on futures contracts if they anticipate a favorable market evolution, but do not want to expose themselves to risk. On the other hand, if the beneficiary has information that the market will have an unfavorable trend for him, he will probably only engage in the futures contract.

7.2.1 Interest Rate Contracts

Interest is continuously capitalized, and interest payments are made on a regular basis. Therefore, while futures and option contracts may cover the effect of changes in interest rates on price, in this case, instruments are needed to cover only the interest rate risk itself; considered separated.

To this end, two types of contracts have been created:

1. Swaps involve the exchange of a fixed interest debt with an interest rate instrument variable.
2. Forward interest rate contracts are used to cover unfavorable interest rate developments in the future, even if there is no interest rate debt at the time of closing. Contract.

The execution of *swap contracts* generally involves the existence of an intermediary (usually a commercial bank) who will identify another debtor who wishes to engage in a swap transaction. It should be noted that the two parties involved in the contract do not necessarily have to have different forecasts on the evolution of interest rates. Depending on how the intermediary bank conducts the risk assessment, both contract partners may benefit from a reduction in rates. Interest.

Swaps have the following characteristics:

* Profit margins are very low, both for the intermediary bank and for the companies involved, so they are used only in transactions with very large amounts (generally at least $10 million).
* The maturities and values of the loans contracted by both companies must be the same.
* There is no movement of loans—the difference between the fixed rate and the variable rate is highlighted without changing the credit risks of debtors.
* The total benefit, for all parties involved, is 85 basis points, i.e., the difference between the fixed rate and that variable.

The gain from the swap transaction is the result of the separation of interest flows from the credit itself. This separation allows companies that do not have access to the capital market to take out loans at variable interest rates and pay fixed interest rates. In addition, due to the flexibility of swap transactions, the company may enter into a contract of equal value, but in the opposite direction, provided there is a counterparty. This process allows you to make a profit when interest rates change significantly.

The term variable interest rate in this case has a special meaning, because it is usually an interest rate set for a certain period, such as LIBOR for 3 months. Thus, the established LIBOR rate is fixed for a period of

3 months. Because of this, payments for swap transactions (PLs) are made at the end of the period for which the floating rate has been set, at a value calculated after the following formula

$$PL = (fixed\ rate - variable\ rate) \times period$$
$$/ 360 \times nominal\ value\ of\ the\ swap\ contract.$$

Forward swap is a classic swap contract that will start at some point in the future, but whose conditions are currently set. For example, a company that intends to enter into a swap agreement in the future, but who estimates that the interest rate will be higher at that time, will be able to enter into a forward swap agreement in order to benefit from the current interest conditions.

The fixed interest rate is higher in the case of a forward swap contract compared to a classic swap contract traded at the same time, due to the yield curve. As there is a risk that the interest rate will be even higher in the future, the company may prefer to enter into a forward swap contract.

The forward swap contract can also be used if there is a short period of time between its term of employment and that of the swap contract (several months), and this contract precedes the issuance of bonds that will be the subject of the swap contract. Before issuing, as part of a broader financial strategy, the company wants to benefit from the current interest conditions for a contract. Swap.

Swap option (swaption) is similar, in principle, to a forward swap contract, except that one of the parties has the right to decide whether to enter a swap contract within a certain period. If the contract is not exercised within a certain period, the beneficiary of the option loses the right he has. Obviously, in order to obtain this right, the beneficiary will pay a first.

Callable swap is a first type of contract derived from the three variants of using a swap option operation. Under a callable swap agreement, the party making the fixed payments (and having the debt incurred at a variable interest rate) has the option of of end the contract swap in the anything moment; from all other puncture of view the contract is a classic one. The existence of this possibility is advantageous in the conditions in which the interest rates decrease significantly, the interest on the debt contracted at a variable rate becoming smaller.

For the flexibility offered by this type of contract, a fixed interest rate premium is applied. Closing the swap contract is often done by making the final payment. If it is estimated that the decrease in interest rates is only temporary, the right to close the swap contract will not be exercised.

Puttable swap is the second type of swap option derivative contract, which offers the party making the variable payments (and has a fixed interest rate obligation) the opportunity to terminate the swap contract at any time. The termination clause will be exercised in the event that interest rates have increased significantly, and it is estimated that they will remain at that level for the entire remaining period of the swap contract. Obviously, in this case too, a premium is paid for the acquisition of this right and there will also be payment the final.

Extendible swap—the third type of contract derived from the swap option—offers the party who pays a fixed interest rate (and has contracted the loan at a variable rate) the possibility to extend the swap contract in the same conditions.

As with previous swap contracts, the core contract is a classic swap. Negotiating additional facilities involves a slightly higher fixed interest rate than in the case of a simple contract.

If the party paying a fixed rate can negotiate a new swap contract at the expiration of the first one, this type of option is attractive if the companies estimate that, in the long run, the rates will be significantly higher than at the time of negotiating the original contract. A new swap contract would involve a higher base rate, and the fixed rate could be significantly higher than the reduced interest rate increases through a swap contract. Obviously, if the interest rates are not higher at the time the initial contract expires, the option is not exercised.

Zero coupon/variable interest swap—is a variant of a classic swap contract in which fixed interest payments are replaced by a single payment at the end of the swap contract. Variable interest payments remain unchanged.

This type of contract may be attractive to a zero-coupon bondholder who estimates interest rates lower and who prefers to reduce variable interest payments. in the exchange receipt of a amounts fixed to conclusion contract swap, protecting and thus, the fixed debt. In such a contract, the partner estimates the interest rate increase.

Rate capped swap—is a contract similar to the previous one; In this case, however, the variable interest payments are limited to a certain maximum interest rate, agreed upon. Thus, in return for the payment of a premium, the party that has incurred a debt at a fixed interest rate limits its exposure to the increase in the interest rate. Obviously, this means that the amounts received by the party who has contracted a debt at a variable rate will not increase if the payments to settle that debt exceed a certain level. Thus, the coverage offered by the swap contract is not perfect. However, the parties may consider this risk to be acceptable, and on the other hand it may not be possible to exceed the maximum interest rate. Significant.

Equity swap does not involve the exchange of shares, but is a swap in which the variable rate is determined by the performance of a specific stock index. For example, change a fixed rate with a Standard & Poor's' appreciation rate 500.

Thus, the rate of increase of the index in each quarter is determined and it is applied at the nominal value for the establishment of the variable interest payments. This type of swap will be used by portfolio managers who estimate that the stock market will grow at a faster rate than the interest rate, but do not want to expose themselves to capital risk and the costs of rescheduling their investments.

Currency options are frequently used in hedging operations. Although they are used for speculative transactions, they are more expensive than futures contracts and that is why they are not so popular. Most foreign exchange options are used to hedge the real currency risk, being issued on the over-the-counter market, especially by banks. In most cases, an option is an alternative to a forward contract if a favorable exchange rate evolution is anticipated, allowing for profit. An option is more expensive than a forward contract; thus, if the risk of loss is anticipated to be low, the forward contract is a better option advantageous.

As mentioned above, the options can be: buy (call option), or sell (put option).

7.3 CALL Option

A CALL contract gives its buyer the right, but not the obligation, to purchase an underlying asset at a certain price, called the exercise price, until or at maturity, in exchange for a premium.

Elements of a CALL option contract

counter	Position in the contract	Position on the underlying asset	Pay / collect the exercise price (PE)	Pay / collect premium (c)
Buyer	Long a	Long a	- ON	- c
Seller	Short	Short	+ PE	+ c

Remarks

1. The buyer of the option relies on the increase of the share price; therefore, he adopts a long position on the asset of support.
2. The seller of the contract relies on the decrease of the price of the action, so that the buyer abandons the option and therefore he collects first.
3. The seller of the option always submits to the buyer's decision to exercise or abandon the contract.
4. The first is paid at the time of closing contract.

In the following, we will use the following notations:

ST—spot price of the action at the end of the contract.
PE—strike price of the option.
PM—*breakeven point* or the point at which the investor neither loses nor gains.

Payoff option—the result of the investor without considering the initial cost (premium).
RT—the final result of the investor at the maturity of the option.

a) In the case of the *buyer* of the CALL contract: The payoff of an option is form

$$Payoff_{T,Long\ CALL} = \begin{cases} S_T - PE, S_T > PE \\ 0, S_T < PE \end{cases} = \max(S_T - PE, 0)$$

The end result, which can be profit or loss, is:

$$R_{T,Long\ Call} = \begin{cases} S_T - PE - c \cdot (1+r), S_T > PE \\ -c \cdot (1+r), S_T < PE \end{cases}$$

In determining the result, the interest rate (r) was also used as the payment of the premium at the end contract implant a cost of opportunity, that of use the amount of money afferent the first during the performance of the option contract. In other words, the time value of a is considered money.

Determination of Dead Centre

When $S_T > PE$, it is observed that the result of the investor is a function that depends on the spot price from the maturity of the action. Therefore, we will equal the result with 0 and we get:

$S_T - PE - c \cdot (1 + r) = 0$
$PM = PE + c \cdot (1 + r)$

b) In the case of the seller of the CALL contract, the payoff of an option is form:
The end result, which can be profit or loss, is:

$$Payoff_{T,Short\ CALL} = \begin{cases} S_T - PE, S_T > PE \\ 0, S_T < PE \end{cases} = -\max(S_T - PE, 0)$$

$$R_{T,Short\ Call} = \begin{cases} S_T - PE + c \cdot (1+r), S_T > PE \\ +c \cdot (1+r), S_T < PE \end{cases}$$

The dead center in the case of the call seller is determined by equalizing the result with zero, on the interval.

$S_T > PE$, $S_T - PE + c \cdot (1 + r) = 0$

Obviously, the deadlock is the same since when the buyer wins, the seller loses and vice versa. So,

$PM = PE + c \cdot (1 + r)$

7.4 PUT Option

A PUT contract confers on its buyer the right but not the obligation to sell an underlying asset at the exercise price, until or at maturity, in exchange for payment of a prime.

Characteristics of a PUT option contract

Counterpart	Position in the contract	Position on the underlying asset	Pay / collect the exercise price (PE)	Pay / collect premium (p)
Buyer	Long	Short	+PE	-p
Short	Long	Seller	-PE	+p

Remarks

1. As in the case of CALL options, the premium is paid at the time of concluding the contract, and the seller of the option always submits to the buyer's decision to exercise or abandon the contract.
2. The buyer of the option bets on the decrease of the share price, therefore he adopts a short position on the asset support.
3. The seller relies on increasing the price of the stock, so that the buyer abandons the option and therefore he collects first.

7 Derivatives

(a) In the case of the *buyer* of the contract WELL.
The payoff of an option, at maturity, is as follows:

$$Payoff_{T,Long\ PUT} = \begin{cases} PE - S_T, S_T < PE \\ 0, S_T > PE \end{cases} = \max(PE - S_T, 0)$$

The final result at maturity, which can be profit or loss, is:

$$R_{T,Long\ PUT} = \begin{cases} PE - S_T - p \cdot (1+r), S_T < PE \\ -p \cdot (1+r), S_T > PE \end{cases}$$

The deadlock is determined as in the case of the call option by matching the result when it depends of the Commercials to maturity with zero. So, the point dead is determined on range $S_T > PE$ and will be:

$$PE - S_T - p \cdot (1+r) = 0$$
$$PM = PE - p \cdot (1+r)$$

(b) In the case of the contract *seller* WELL.
The payoff and the end result for the well seller are described by the relationships:

$$Payoff_{T,Short\ PUT} = \begin{cases} S_T - PE, S_T < PE \\ 0, S_T > PE \end{cases} = -\max(PE - S_T, 0)$$

$$R_{T,Short\ PUT} = \begin{cases} S_T - PE + p \cdot (1+r), S_T < PE \\ p \cdot (1+r), S_T > PE \end{cases}$$

The deadlock in the case of a well sale is similar to that of the well purchase, and the payoff and the final result.

7.5 Option Strategies

This section presents the main strategies that a market operator, an investor can adopt depending on the purpose pursued, namely hedging strategies of an open position in the spot market, spread strategies aimed at limiting a loss or strategies combined with call and put options based on low/high volatility expectations of asset price support.

7.5.1 Strategies for Hedge

These can be built with options to avoid possible losses when holding a long position on a stock. The most used hedging strategies are protective put and covered call.

Protective Put
If an investor holds a long position on a share, then he is exposed to the risk of the share price falling below the price at which it was bought. Thus, in order to remove these losses, when the shares are bought (S0), a long position will be adopted on a put option contract (PE), as it is in-the-money when the price falls below exercise price. As a rule, the exercise price is lower than the share price. Below is how the strategy is deduced, considering the value of time a money.

Protective

Trader position	$0 < S_T < PE$ strategy put	$S_T > PE$
Long stock	$S_T - S_0 \cdot (1+r)$	$S_T - S_0 \cdot (1+r)$
Long Put at PE	$PE - S_T - p \cdot (1+r)$	$-p \cdot (1+r)$
Result	$C = PE - (1+r) \cdot (S_0 + p)$	$S_T - (1+r) \cdot (S_0 + p)$

Covered Call

As an alternative to the put protection strategy, investors who have a long position in a stock are exposed to the risk of lowering its price. To limit any losses, when buying shares, the investor will take a short position on a call option.

Covered

Trader position	$0 < S_T < PE$ call strategy	$S_T > PE$
Long stock Short Call la PE	$S_T - S_0 \cdot (1+r)$ $c \cdot (1+r)$	$S_T - S_0 \cdot (1+r)$ $PE - S_T + c \cdot (1+r)$
Strategy result	$C = S_T - (1+r) \cdot (S_0 - c)$	$PE - (1+r) \cdot (S_0 - c)$

In the case of the putty protection strategy, it is observed that the loss becomes limited, and if the investor's fears do not come true, the profit will be reduced fixedly with the premium initially paid (at maturity this is valid)s $p \cdot (1 + r)$. The same is true for the covered call strategy, profiteer reducing to.

$$PE - (1+r) \cdot (S_0 - c)$$

7.5.2 Options Trading Strategies on Spread

Option transactions that consist of the simultaneous sale and purchase of two or more options of the same type with the intention of profiting from price developments are called spreads.

The purpose of a spread transaction is to establish a position in the options market so that the loss is limited. As with other strategies, a trader anticipates a certain evolution of the price of the underlying asset. Spread strategies can be used when anticipating a growing market called a bull spread strategy or anticipating a bear market. But there are also strategies such as butterfly and condor that can be earned, whether the market is growing or the market is declining.

Bull Spread

One of the most popular strategies is bull spread. This can be created using either call or put options. If call options with the same maturity and the same underlying asset are used, the strategy is as follows:

* Purchase option call (long call) on asset support to a price of exercise PE 1, received c1
* Call option (short call) on the same medium at an exercise price of PE 2, first c 2; (PE 1 < PE 2)

Since the price of the call option (decrease) always decreases as the exercise price increases, the value of the option sold is lower than that of the option purchased (c 2 < c 1).

Usually, the bull spread strategy is built by a trader who anticipates the increase of the share price, but at the same time, he wants to limit his loss. Below, the strategy is deduced from the options used.

Bull spread strategy using call options

Trader position	$0 < S_T < PE_1$	$PE_1 < S_T < PE_2$	$S_T > PE_2$
Long Call la PE_1	$-c_1$	$ST - PE_1 - c_1$	$ST - PE_1 - c_1$
Short Call la PE_2	c_2	c_2	$PE_2 - S_T + c_2$
	$-c_1 + c_2$	$ST - PE_1 - c_1 + c_2$	$PE_2 - PE_1 - c_1 + c_2$

It is observed that the dead center is: $PE_1 + c_1 - c_2$. At the same time, it is observed that indeed the loss is limited to $-c_1 + c_2$, but also the profit is limited, respectively $PE_2 - PE_1 - c_1 + c_2$.

Bear Spread

It was noticed that a trader who adopts a bull spread strategy anticipates that the market is growing. Conversely, in the case of a bear spread strategy, the trader anticipates a market in decrease.

Using call options with the same maturity and the same support asset, the strategy is formed as follows:

- Call option (short call) on the same medium at an exercise price of PE 1, the first c 1
- Purchase option call (long call) on asset support to a price of exercise PE 2, received c2; (PE 1 < PE 2). As in the previous case c2 < c1

The strategy obtained is presented below.

Bear spread strategy using call options

Trader position	$0 < S_T < PE_1$	$PE_1 < S_T < PE_2$	$S_T > PE_2$
Short Call la PE_1	c_1	$PE_1 - S_T + c_1$	$ST - PE_1 - c_1$
Long Call la PE_2	$-c_2$	$-c_2$	$PE_2 - S_T + c_2$
	$c_1 - c_2$	$PE_1 - S_T + c_1 - c_2$	$PE_1 - PE_2 + c_1 - c_2$

This strategy makes a profit when the price of the underlying asset falls below neutral limited the $c_1 - c_2$. Otherwise, when the rate rises above neutral, the loss is limited ($PE_1 - PE_2 + c_1 - c_2$).

Condor

Such a strategy allows a greater flexibility of an investor's anticipation regarding the evolution of the price of the underlying asset. Thus, the condor strategy will be profitable either when the price of the underlying asset increases or when it falls below the corresponding dead center. Like any spread strategy, the condor will consist of four options of the same type, call or well with the same support asset, the same maturity, different positions. Suppose an investor has the following options in his portfolio:

- A long position on a call contract, having $PE_1 = 70$ USD, $c_1 = 9$;
- A position short on a contract call with $PE_2 = 75$ USD, $c_2 = 6$ USD;
- A position short on a contract call with $PE_3 = 80$ USD, $c_3 = 4$ USD;
- A long position on a call contract $PE_4 = 85$ USD, $c_4 = \$ 2$.

The size of a contract is $ 100, the number of contracts is 10 on each open position, contracts have the same underlying asset and the same maturity. As in the previous cases, the relationship between the primes will be: c 1 > c 2 > c 3 > c 4. The table below shows the results for all four options at different intervals in which the underlying asset price would fall, as well as the strategy obtained.

Condor strategy using call options

T r	$0 < S_T < PE_1$	$PE_1 < S_T < PE_2$	$PE_2 < S_T < PE_3$	$PE_3 < S_T < PE_4$	$S_T > PE_4$
1 LC PE_1 1 SC PE_2 1 SC PE_3	$-c_1$ c_2 $-c_3$ $-c_4$	$S_T - PE_1 - c_1$ c_2 c_3 $-c_4$	$S_T - PE_1 - c_1$ $PE_2 - S_T + c_2$ c_3 $-c_4$	$S_T - PE_1 - c_1$ $PE_2 - S_T + c_2$ $PE_3 - S_T + c_3$ $-c_4$	$ST - PE_1 - c_1$ $PE_2 - S_T + c_2$ $PE_3 - S_T + c_3$ $ST - PE_4 - c_4$
	C	$S_T - PE_1 + C$	$PE_2 - PE_1 + C$	$-S_T - PE_1 + PE_2 + PE_3 + C$	$PE_2 - PE_1 + PE_3 - P$

We note the strategy cost C: $C = -c_1 + c_2 + c_3 - c_4 = -1$ USD
We notice that the strategy becomes:

	$0 < S_T < PE_1$	$PE_1 < S_T < PE_2$	$PE_2 < S_T < PE_3$	$PE_3 < S_T < PE_4$	$S_T > PE_4$
Strategy result	-1	$S_T - 71$	4	$84 - S_T$	-1

The example shown shows:

- Through a strategy the loss is limited to the interval

$$S_T \in (0, PE_1) \cup (PE_4, \infty)$$

$$\text{Loss} = -1 \cdot 10 \text{contracts} \cdot 100 \frac{\text{USD}}{\text{contract}} = -1000 \text{USD}$$

- The profit is limited, the maximum profit being:

$$\text{Profit} = 4 \cdot 10 \text{contracts} \cdot 100 \frac{\text{USD}}{\text{contract}} = 4000 \text{USD}$$

It can be won when the price of the stock is between (71, 80), so when it increases, but also when the price decreases from 84 USD to 80 USD.

7.5.3 Strategies Using Combinations of Call and Options Put

Straddle

It is a strategy that can be formed using a call option and a put option with the same maturity, the same support asset and exercise price. The one who will bet on a high volatility of the course will opt for a long straddle, instead the one who will anticipate a low volatility will adopt a short straddle strategy. The following tables illustrate the two strategies.

Long straddle strategy

Trader position	$0 < PE < S_T$	$S_T > PE$
Long Call la PE	$-c \cdot (1+r)$	$S_T - PE - c \cdot (1+r)$
Long Put la PE	$PE - S_T - p \cdot (1+r)$	$-p \cdot (1+r)$
Strategy result	$PE - S_T - (c+p) \cdot (1+r)$	$S_T - PE - (c+p) \cdot (1+r)$

Short straddle strategy

Strategy position	$0 < PE < S_T$	$S_T > PE$
Short Call la PE	$c \cdot (1+r)$	$PE - S_T + c \cdot (1+r)$
Short Put la PE	$S_T - PE + p \cdot (1+r)$	$p \cdot (1+r)$
Strategy result	$S_T - PE + (c+p) \cdot (1+r)$	$PE - S_T + (c+p) \cdot (1+r)$

The dead center will be $PM_1 = PE - (c+p) \cdot (1+r)$, when $0 < PE < ST$, respectively $PM_2 = PE + (c+p) \cdot (1+r)$, when $ST > ON$.

It is noted that in the case of the straddle buyer the loss will be limited and is maximum when the price of the underlying asset would be equal to the exercise price. Profit is limited when the price of the underlying asset falls below PM 1, or unlimited when it rises above PM 2.

Strangle

As in the case of the straddle strategy, call and put options will be used with the same underlying asset, the same maturity, but the exercise price will be different (that of the put option will be lower than that of the call option).

Trader position	$0 < S_T < PE_1$	$PE_1 < S_T < PE_2$	$S_T > PE_2$
Short Call la PE_1			
Long Call la PE_2			
Result	$PE_1 - S_T - p \cdot (1+r)$ $-c \cdot (1+r)$	$-p \cdot (1+r)$ $-c \cdot (1+r)$	$-p \cdot (1+r)$ $S_T - PE_2 - c \cdot (1+r)$
strategy	$PE_1 - S_T - (c+p) \cdot (1+r)$	$-(c+p) \cdot (1+r)$	$S_T - PE_2 - (c+p) \cdot (1+r)$

Unlike straddle, the buyer's loss in this strategy will be limited in the range (PE 1, PE 2), not in a single point, and in the case of the seller, the profit will be limited in the range (PE 1, PE 2).

The dead points are: $PM_1 = PE_1 - (c + p) \cdot (1 + r)$, when $0 < PE_1 < S_T$, respectively $PM_2 = PE_2 + (c + p) \cdot (1 + r)$, when $S_T > PE_2$.

Strips and Straps are variants of the straddle strategy. A strip strategy consists of two positions on a put contract and one position on a call contract, having the same support asset and exercise price, the same maturity. A strap strategy consists of two positions on a call contract and one position on a put contract.

8

Summary Problems

1. Calculate the profitability of an action whose initial value is 0.25 lei and with a final value of 0.35 lei, knowing that at the end of the year, a dividend of 0.05 lei was paid.

   (a) $R_i = 0.5$
   (b) $R_i = 0.4$
   (c) $R_i = 0.6$
   (d) $R_i = 0.8$

Solution
We will use the formula:

$$R_i = \frac{P_1 - P_0 + D}{P_0}$$

$$R_i = \frac{0.35 - 0.25 + 0.05}{0.25}$$

$$R_i = \frac{0.15}{0.25}$$

$$R_i = 0.6$$

2. Calculate the profitability of a stock whose initial value is 0.2 lei and with a final value of 0.3 lei, knowing that at the end of the year, no dividend was paid.

(a) $R_i = 0.5$
(b) $R_i = 0$
(c) $R_i = 1.5$
(d) $R_i = 0.4$

Solution
We will use the formula:

$$R_i = \frac{P_1 - P_0 + D}{P_0}$$

$$R_i = \frac{0.3 - 0.2 + 0}{0.2}$$

$$R_i = \frac{0.1}{0.2}$$

$$R_i = 0.5$$

3. An asset brought, for 3 years, the annual dividends of 4 lei, 5 lei and 6 lei and is resold at 3 years from the date of purchase at the price of 121 lei. To find out the price at which the stock was bought, if the annual rate of evaluation of its rate was 5%.
    We know: $D_1 = 4$ lei, $D_2 = 5$ lei, $D_3 = 6$ lei, $C_3 = 121$ lei.

(a) $C_0 = 118.05$
(b) $C_0 = 136.07$
(c) $C_0 = 108.09$
(d) $C_0 = 86.15$

Solution

$$C_0 = \frac{D_1}{(1+i)} + \frac{D_2}{(1+i)^2} + \frac{D_3+C_3}{(1+i)^3} = \frac{4}{(1.05)} + \frac{5}{(1.05)^2} + \frac{6+121}{(1.05)^3}$$

$$C_0 = 118.05$$

4. We consider that two assets are listed on the market with returns $E(R_1) = E(R_2) = 0, 1$ and risks $\sigma_1 = 0, 15$, $\sigma_2 = 0, 25$. The two assets evolve independently in the market, i.e., the correlation coefficient between the two assets is $\rho_{12} = 0$. Determine the covariance between the two assets and write the covariance variance matrix.

(a) $\Omega = \begin{pmatrix} 0.0125 & 0 \\ 0 & 0.0225 \end{pmatrix}$

(b) $\Omega = \begin{pmatrix} 0.0225 & 0 \\ 0 & 0.0625 \end{pmatrix}$

(c) $\Omega = \begin{pmatrix} 0.225 & 0 \\ 0 & 0.625 \end{pmatrix}$

(d) $\Omega = \begin{pmatrix} 0.125 & 0 \\ 0 & 0.125 \end{pmatrix}$

Solution
We compute the covariance according to the formula: $\sigma_{12} = \rho_{12}\sigma_1\sigma_2 = 0$
the variance-covariance matrix is: $\Omega = \begin{pmatrix} 0.0225 & 0 \\ 0 & 0.0625 \end{pmatrix}$

5. We consider that two assets are listed on the market with returns $\mu = \begin{pmatrix} E(R_1) \\ E(R_2) \end{pmatrix} = \begin{pmatrix} 0.1 \\ 0.2 \end{pmatrix}$ and risks $\sigma_1 = 0.2$, $\sigma_2 = 0.3$. The correlation coefficient between the two assets is $\rho_{12} = -1$. Determine the covariance between the two assets and write the covariance variance matrix.

(a) $\Omega = \begin{pmatrix} 0.06 & -0.012 \\ -0.012 & 0.09 \end{pmatrix}$

(b) $\Omega = \begin{pmatrix} 0.4 & -0.6 \\ -0.6 & 0.9 \end{pmatrix}$

(c) $\Omega = \begin{pmatrix} 0.006 & -0.016 \\ -0.016 & 0.09 \end{pmatrix}$

(d) $\Omega = \begin{pmatrix} 0.04 & -0.06 \\ -0.06 & 0.09 \end{pmatrix}$

Solution

We compute the covariance with the formula: $\sigma_{12} = \rho_{12}\sigma_1\sigma_2 = -0.06$

The variance-covariance matrix is: $\Omega = \begin{pmatrix} 0.04 & -0.06 \\ -0.06 & 0.09 \end{pmatrix}$

6. We consider a market stock (i). The return of stock (i), in the time range from $t = 0$ to $t = 1$, is denoted by (R_i) and has the following distribution:

$$R_i : \begin{pmatrix} 0.2 & 0.3 & 0.2 & 0.2 & 0.1 \\ 1.4 & 1.5 & 1.5 & 1.4 & 1.4 \end{pmatrix}.$$

The return of the stock is:

(a) $E(R_i) = 1.50$
(b) $E(R_i) = 1.55$
(c) $E(R_i) = 1.45$
(d) $E(R_i) = 1.65$

Solution
Return of the stock:

$$E(R_i) = \sum_{k=1}^{n} p_k \cdot R_{ik},$$ where p_k and R_k were previously defined.

Thus, we get:

$$E(R_i) = 0.2 \cdot 1.4 + 0.3 \cdot 1.5 + 0.2 \cdot 1.5 + 0.2 \cdot 1.4 + 0.1 \cdot 1.4$$

$$E(R_i) = 1.45$$

7. We consider an action (R_i) in the five possible future states:

$$R_i : \begin{pmatrix} 0.2 & 0.3 & 0.2 & 0.2 & 0.1 \\ 1.4 & 1.5 & 1.5 & 1.4 & 1.4 \end{pmatrix}$$

Compute the risk of the stock.

(a) $\sigma_i = 8\%$
(b) $\sigma_i = 1\%$
(c) $\sigma_i = 9\%$
(d) $\sigma_i = 5\%$

Solution

$$E(R_i^2) = \sum_{k=1}^{n} p_k \cdot R^2_{\,k}$$

$$E(R_i^2) = 0.2 \cdot 1.4^2 + 0.3 \cdot 1.5^2 + 0.2 \cdot 1.5^2 + 0.2 \cdot 1.4^2 + 0.1 \cdot 1.4^2$$

$$E(R_i^2) = 1.5562$$

The variance is:

$$\sigma_i^2 = \text{var}(R_i) = E(R_i^2) - E(R_i)^2$$

$$= 1.5562 - 1.45^2$$

$$= 2.22 - 1.45^2$$

$$= 2.105 - 2.1025$$

$$= 0.0025$$

The risk is: $\sigma_i = \sqrt{0.0025} = 0.05 = 5\%$

8. We consider a portfolio consisting of two shares R_1 and R_2. R_1 has the return $E(R_1) = 20\%$ and the risk $\sigma_1 = 8\%$, and R_2 it has the return $E(R_2) = 30\%$ and the risk $\sigma_2 = 9\%$. We consider a portfolio $w = (w_1, w_2)$, where w_1 and w_2 represents the portfolio weights of each share: $w_1 = 40\%$, $w_2 = 60\%$ and $\rho_{12} = -1$.
Compute the return of the portfolio.

(a) $E(R_p) = 0.46$
(b) $E(R_p) = 0.26$
(c) $E(R_p) = 0.16$
(d) $E(R_p) = 0.18$

Solution
We denote with R_p the portfolio obtained from the two actions. This portfolio consists of w_1 of the first stock and w_2 the second. Then:

$$R_p = x_1 \cdot R_1 + x_2 \cdot R_2$$

8 Summary Problems

For this portfolio, we will compute the return:

$$E(R_p) = x_1 \cdot E(R_1) + x_2 \cdot E(R_2)$$

By plugging in the numbers, we get:

$$E(R_p) = x_1 \cdot 0.20 + x_2 \cdot 0.30$$
$$E(R_p) = 0.4 \cdot 0.2 + 0.6 \cdot 0.3$$
$$E(R_p) = 0.26$$

9. Compute the risk of the portfolio in the previous problem.

   (a) $\sigma^2_{R_p} = 0.000484$

   (b) $\sigma^2_{R_p} = 0.00684$

   (c) $\sigma^2_{R_p} = 0.464$

   (d) $\sigma^2_{R_p} = 0.00424$

Solution

$$\sigma^2_{R_p} = (x_1)^2 \cdot \sigma_1^2 + (x_2)^2 \cdot \sigma_1^2 + 2(x_1)(x_2)\rho_{12}\sigma_1\sigma_2$$

$$\sigma^2_{R_p} = (0.4)^2 \cdot (0.08)^2 + (0.6)^2 \cdot (0.09)^2 + 2(0.4)(0.6)\rho_{12}(0.08)(0.09)$$

$$\sigma^2_{R_p} = 0.001024 + 0.002916 + 0.003456 \cdot \rho_{12}$$

$$\sigma^2_{R_p} = 0.00394 + 0.003456 \cdot (-1)$$

$$\sigma^2_{R_p} = 0.000484$$

10. We consider a three-stock portfolio with the following weights: $w_1 = 50\%$, $w_2 = 30\%$, $w_3 = 20\%$. The return of the portfolio is:

(a) $E(R_p) = -0.144$
(b) $E(R_p) = 0.144$
(c) $E(R_p) = 0.134$
(d) $E(R_p) = 0.124$

Solution
We have: $w^T = (0.5; 0.3; 0.2)$
The return of the portfolio is:

$$E(R_p) = w_1 \cdot E(R_1) + w_2 \cdot E(R_2) + w_3 \cdot E(R_3)$$

By plugging in the numbers, we get:

$$E(R_p) = (0.5) \cdot 0.12 + (0.3) \cdot 0.14 + (0.2) \cdot 0.16$$

$$E(R_p) = 0.134$$

Printed in the United States
by Baker & Taylor Publisher Services